The Price of Leadership

Ellyn Lerner, PhD

School Realty, LP

The Price of Leadership
Copyright © 2011 Ellyn Lerner, PhD
Published by School Realty, LP

For more information please contact EllynLerner@aol.com

Book design by Arbor Books, Inc.
www.arborbooks.com

Printed in the United States of America

The Price of Leadership
Ellyn Lerner, Ph.D.

1. Title   2. Author   3. Memoir

Library of Congress Control Number: 2010913072

ISBN 13: 978-0-615-40083-9

To my husband Alan and my daughters Melissa and Erica

Preface

The story in this book is true, and I have told it as honestly as I can. In some instances, I have recreated scenes and conversations to the best of my ability, based on evidence and my own recollections. In addition, I have changed the names of the two New Road accounting staff members involved in the legal proceedings described herein and the name of one other school-level person.

Prologue

April 19, 2004. A Monday. A workday. At eight in the morning I pulled into the parking lot of the New Road School in Parlin, New Jersey—my workplace, my baby, my life—expecting to park my car, go inside and get down to the business of running things. Just like any other day of the week.

The school wasn't actually open yet, so there would be no kids around and few other adults—only a handful of administrative staff and myself. So far, this was just a half-empty building but soon, it would be a state-of-the-art facility for the education and vocational training of kids with special needs, a population I'd devoted more than half my life to by that point. Lately I'd been splitting my days between the central office here in Parlin and our other new school in Somerset, supervising the contractors and making sure that everything got built to my specifications. New Road was part of a network of several other schools, but these two would be our flagship facilities and I took great pride in being the driving force behind them.

In the parking lot, I saw the few, familiar cars of the other early birds I worked with and—*strangely*—a gaggle of gray and black Crown Victorias crowded around the building's entrance like a flock of hungry geese. I stopped my car and looked at them. Had something happened? An emergency? Why hadn't I been notified? Maybe there was a meeting I'd forgotten about, or an inspection I'd neglected to pencil into my date book. Even worse, it could have been a *surprise* inspection. That was one problem with running a state-funded facility—they could just show up whenever they wanted to, whether you were ready to see them or not. That sort of thing led to code violations, to fines, to delays in construction, in permits, in opening. In a moment, I was thinking the worst.

I pulled quickly into my usual parking spot and ran toward the school's entrance, anxious to find out what was going on inside. In the lobby, I looked around for signs of commotion—an accident, an injury, a flood, a blackout—hoping that some emergency *had* summoned that posse of governmental-looking cars to my school. But there was nothing. No employees on stretchers, no furniture on fire, no collapsed ceilings. Everything seemed peaceful, in order, bright and sunny. Nothing appeared to be wrong.

So, I headed to my office, hoping that someone there would be able to explain. In those days we worked out of some rooms on the lower level of the building while the contractors worked on the school's main and second floors above us. I expected that when I got down there, everything would be normal. I'd see Kathy, my assistant, and Jill, our receptionist, and whichever of the accounting girls had made it in already, and they would tell me why all those cars were there. And then, at least I would know and I could start to deal with it.

But on the lower level, I found myself completely alone. No Kathy, no Jill, no chatting and laughing bookkeepers. The place was silent except for the hum of the fluorescent lights, the only sign of life. I felt like I'd stumbled onto the set of some nuclear-war-aftermath horror flick, and it made my skin crawl. This was supposed to be my workplace, the central office, the hub of everything. So, where were all the people?

"Hello?" I called, my own echo the only reply.

I ran into my newly built-out office and dropped my briefcase down on the desk, then picked up my phone, thinking of who I could call to get some answers. Dave, my co-CEO? Maybe, but he was still on his way in. If I didn't know anything, chances were he didn't either. Mark, the CFO? No, he probably hadn't even left home yet. I allowed him to stagger his hours so he would miss the rush hour; he lived all the way out in Pennsylvania and had a rough commute as it was. He rarely made an appearance before nine-thirty.

As I pondered the situation, out of nowhere, a voice called out to me.

"Ellyn Lerner?" it barked from down the hall, scaring me half to death, and I dropped the phone receiver. I waited, listening to a set of heavy footsteps make its way across the basement, through the maze of rooms and over to my doorway. It was a police officer—toweringly tall, angry-looking and full of muscles, the sort of guy you see on those "unbelievable videos" shows using excessive force to subdue a suspect.

"Ellyn Lerner?" he repeated in his deep voice. "You'll have to come with me."

A cop. And I had to go with him. Had I done something wrong? Or one of my employees? Maybe everyone had evacuated the building because of some safety hazard—asbestos or mold, something the contractors had uncovered. Would the police get involved for something like that? Or was it something more serious? Had someone died? Been killed? Been caught selling drugs? In the absence of any real information, my mind jumped—again—to all sorts of crazy conclusions.

"Uh…excuse me?" I asked him, trying not to sound as frightened as I felt. "What's going on here, Officer?"

He took a deep breath and just looked at me for a moment, then leveled his gaze and put his hands on his utility belt. A little too close to his sidearm, I thought. Was he trying to intimidate me? Did he really think that he would have to draw his weapon on a small-framed, five-foot-three, fifty-something-year-old woman? And in suburbia, no less. This sort of thing just didn't happen there. Not in my life, anyway.

"Step away from the desk, ma'am," he said sternly, moving toward me, "and away from that computer. Don't want you deleting any files." When I didn't move, he repeated himself, this time more loudly. "Step *away*," he warned. "I won't ask you again."

I shook my head, not believing what I was hearing. "What?" I asked, though I instinctively did step back, away from the desk, as he approached. "*Why?*"

"Ma'am," he said once more, "you'll have to come with me," and with that he reached a hand out toward me. Taking my elbow so roughly I was sure I'd be bruised by the next morning, he led me past our newly furnished conference room, away from all the other offices and toward the stairs.

"This way," he said, letting go of my arm and gesturing upwards.

"What's going on here? Where is everybody?" I asked him as I went up, regaining a bit of my composure. I still wanted some answers, wanted to know where my employees were, what those cop cars outside were about. But again, he didn't answer me. He only grabbed my elbow once more and steered me down the hallway, staying one step behind me like I was a criminal being led to my prison cell. At the time, this seemed like an amusing analogy.

"Where *is* everybody?" I asked again, stopping for a moment and jerking my arm out of his grip. I tried to stare him down—or, rather, up, at his height—and I put my hands on my hips, giving him the best stern schoolteacher look I could muster. Though it had been a while since I'd stood in front of a classroom, I thought I still knew a few ways to get a kid to answer me.

But no luck. Instead of telling me what I wanted to know, he simply gazed off over my head, down the hallway. I sighed, resigning myself to the fact that I was not going to get any information from him, and turned to look as well, to see what on earth could have been so fascinating.

And that, as they say in the movies, was when everything went horribly wrong.

Down the hallway from where we stood, a team of men and women emerged from seemingly nowhere—suits, bullet-proof vests, badges hanging from their necks or clipped on their lapels, they looked for the life of them just like the cast of *Law & Order*. Each carried a lidded cardboard box, labeled on the sides in black Sharpie: EVIDENCE, and the name of the school.

For a moment, I just stared at them, my mouth hanging open. *Badges?* I thought, my mind unable, for the moment, to form cohesive thoughts. *Boxes? What's going—*

"What *is* going on here?" I asked the police officer loudly now, whirling around to face him. He looked startled, as though I wasn't meant to see these people. He looked at me, and then at them, then back at me again.

"This way, ma'am," he said again tersely, clamping back on to my elbow. He pulled me hard down the opposite hallway. When we reached the gym door, he pulled it open roughly and practically shoved me inside. "You'll have to wait in here," he told me quickly. "Someone will come and talk to you."

I just stood there for a moment, watching him through the door's narrow window. He ran back down the hallway. I pictured him meeting up with the *Law & Order* folks, telling them that everything was under control, that I was—what? Contained? Out of the way? No longer a threat? I shook my head at the absurdity of it. What on earth was going on here? And when was someone going to give me some answers? "Oh, Ellyn, you made it!" someone said behind me, and I turned to see Kathy, my assistant, running across the gym toward me, her high heels clicking loudly. She looked nearly panicked and for a moment, I felt more concerned about her than anything else.

"Kathy," I said as she approached, smiling at her, trying to calm her down. "Are you okay?"

She nodded a little too hard. "I'm okay," she said. "I'm okay. But what's going on here?"

I continued smiling, not wanting to make her any more upset than she already was. "I don't know," I told her honestly. "But they don't send ten unmarked police cars out for nothing. Something must have happened, maybe overnight while we weren't here. Maybe the contractors came in this morning and found something—I don't know, wrong in some way."

I looked past her, to the other side of the gym, where the rest of the staff sat on folding chairs. Looked like only Jill and the accountants—Sharyn, Michelle and Antoinette—had made it in so far.

Kathy shook her head, again a little bit too vigorously. "I don't know, Ellyn, I don't know," she said nervously. "They won't tell us anything. Fifteen of them came in at once, down on the first floor. At first I thought they were looking for donations for the Police Benevolent Fund or something like that...but then they made us all come in here. That's all I know."

"Well," I said to Kathy, putting a hand on her arm in what I hoped was a reassuring manner. "I was told that someone would come in to talk to me, so let's just try to wait and see what happens."

We went back across the gym and joined the others. They all look so worried; I tried to assure them that everything would be fine, but they knew me too well, and my words were useless. They could tell I was scared just as much as I could see it on all of their faces. Unable to tell them anything good, I felt powerless, at a loss. In the end I just sat down with them and waited for something to happen.

Eventually, someone did come in to talk to me—another police officer, though he didn't really say anything other than, "Dr. Lerner, please stand up." Then, in front of my employees, he escorted me out of the gym, holding me by the elbow like the first guy had. It was embarrassing, to say the least—humiliating, at best. I could only imagine what my staff was trying to make of it.

The officer led me back downstairs, where the crew with the boxes was going to town. Computers had been removed from desks; file drawers were open and even the supply closet had been ransacked. My office, I saw out of the corner of my eye, had a paper banner over the door with the letter "P" on it; Dave's office was marked "R," Kathy's "S" and Mark's "T." The conference room, my final destination on this walk of shame, was labeled as "Q."

Appropriate, I thought. *Q as in question, as in when is anyone going to answer any of mine?*

Inside the conference room, door closed behind me, I paced the floor and bit my nails, waiting for any sort of news or explanation from anyone who was in charge of this thing. But there was nothing. Just a lot of long, empty time and silence. Finally, I flopped down into a chair, knowing there was nothing else I could do. They would only talk to me when they wanted to, and no amount of worrying on my part would change that.

Thirty minutes later, my patience paid off and someone finally did come to speak to me—one of the suit-and-trench-coat squad, a stocky, middle-aged man who badly needed a haircut and a shave. Maybe this whole affair had started too early for him; he certainly looked like he could use another hour or two of sleep.

"Ben Kukis," he said by way of introduction. "And here's your search warrant."

I took it from him, a simple swath of stapled-together papers that, I supposed, explained what he was doing here. "A search warrant?" I asked, looking at it as if it were written in some alien language. "For what? What are you searching for?"

He smiled at me, a smug, patronizing grin that made my skin crawl. "Illegal activity," he replied.

"Wait," I said, holding my hands out in front of me as if that alone could ward off this craziness. "Just wait. Illegal activity? Am I under arrest for something?"

Kukis looked at me, pausing as if trying to make me sweat it. His eyes were bloodshot and humorless. "No," he finally answered slowly, flatly. "You are not."

"Then can I leave?" I asked. "I mean, can I go back to my office? Or the gym? Can I go see my people?"

"No, not yet. We have some questions for you."

Questions? I thought. *About what?* I hadn't done anything illegal. I was an upstanding member of the community, a highly respected educator and businesswoman who had never, *ever* had a problem with the law in my life. I'd never even gotten as much as a speeding ticket. And now this? Now they wanted to detain me and *question* me?

"Am I allowed to call a lawyer first?" I asked him calmly, the idea suddenly popping into my head.

He smirked, reaching into his jacket and pulling out a note pad. "Well, if you didn't do anything wrong," he said, casually flipping through its pages, "and you have nothing to hide, we could just have a friendly chat."

I squinted my eyes at him suspiciously. Nothing about this environment seemed *friendly* to me, and there was no way I was going to *chat* with him about anything. I'd seen those TV shows where people talked to the police and then their entire worlds fell apart. I was not willing to risk my life, my livelihood and above all else my school because of whatever was going on there, and I'd be damned if this miserable little man would rope me into saying anything I'd later regret.

Besides, someone had once told me that if I was ever in trouble, I shouldn't say a word until I had legal representation.

"I want my lawyer first," I told him, because I certainly seemed to be in a lot of trouble at the moment.

One

"Jill," I said to our receptionist as I strode into the office lobby. "Are you ready for judgment day?"

She eyed me over the top of her computer monitor. "Pardon, Dr. Lerner?"

Just past her desk, I stopped abruptly and turned back. "The auditors, Jill," I said with just a bit of exaggerated exasperation. "The financial audit starts today! Don't you remember?"

"Oh, yeah, they're already here!" she told me, not looking quite so frightened now. "They're in the conference room, eating bagels." She leaned toward me a little bit and whispered, "Are you nervous?"

I paused for a moment. Let's see… These people came into our accounting offices for weeks at a time and picked apart every invoice, memo and balance sheet we'd filed in the last year. They poked and they prodded, and they acted like we all worked for them. They got everyone in accounting and bookkeeping running around in a panic and distracted me from my own work in the schools as well.

"Am I nervous?" I repeated back to her, but then grinned and waved my hand dismissively. "Nah, I'm good," I said, walking away again toward my office. "It's all good!"

And that was true, for the most part. In 2003, a full year before all the bad stuff happened—the police raid, the detention, the questioning and everything that came after it—I *was* good most of the time. I was happy. Not so much when I had to be in the office instead of the field, as I had to be on this day, and definitely not during an audit, but even so, I made the best of it. I had a good life, a wonderful family and an excellent career. I had very, very little to complain about and so much for which I felt truly blessed.

"Morning, Mark," I said next, sticking my head into the office of Mark Jeffries, New Road's CFO and the one probably most unnerved by the impending audit. "Got all your ducks in a row? Are your pencils sharpened?"

He looked up at me and just kind of smirked, pulling one corner of his mouth back into a sneer. "They can take my pencils and stick 'em—"

"Whoa, okay, more than I need to know!" I told him, heading off his off-colored metaphor before he could finish it. Mark had been with us for a long time, almost since the beginning, and I was used to his sometimes-brutish demeanor. Today, I thought, I could forgive his surliness but only because I knew what it was like to be in the hot seat; I had to go through program auditing in the schools myself, though that only happened every four or five years and we'd just finished one up in 2002. This financial audit would be time-consuming and cumbersome for Mark and his staff but very little work for me, so I guessed I should be more sympathetic toward him.

"A simple 'yes, Ellyn' would have sufficed," I told him with a gracious smile.

"Yes, Ellyn," he repeated sarcastically, and I retreated back into the hallway before anything more vulgar flew out of his mouth.

I entered my office and dropped my things—briefcase, pocketbook, cell phone—onto the little meeting table just inside the door, then went around to the windows and opened the blinds, checking if my plants needed watering—anything to put off going into the conference room for just a few minutes more.

"Ellyn? Are you coming?"

I jumped a little at the sound of the voice behind me. Turning around, I was greeted by Dave sticking his head through my doorway. Dave was my co-CEO, my partner in this business and the guy who ran the office. He often referred to himself as our "in-house bureaucrat," as he took care of all the rules and regulations while I spent my time out in the field, taking care of the programs. Eight years older than me, salt-and-pepper haired and stoic like nobody's business, to our employees, Dave was sort of an ivory-tower type, a man to be respected, revered and even obeyed. To me, however, he was just an old friend and sparring partner. Our relationship was certainly love/hate, but in the end we got the job done and that was what mattered.

"Morning," I said to him calmly. "I hear the automatons have taken over again."

Dave laughed. "Yes, they're in the conference room, refueling for the next wave of attack. I think they'll be ready to go in a few minutes."

I laughed, too, as I plastered a smile onto my face. This was going to be a long, long six weeks.

—————

It wasn't that I disliked audits. Okay, well, it was—I hated them as much as I hated anything else that took my focus away from the schools and the kids. Audits were tedious and nitpicky, nothing but weeks full of the worst kind of scrutiny. But, with New Road being a state-funded organization, they were a necessary bit of drudgery, something that we had to undergo once a year if I wanted the place to stay in operation. I considered them a small price to pay for getting to continue doing the thing that I loved most. And besides, I had nothing to hide. At least, back then, I didn't think I did.

The audits were the same every time. A bunch of dullards from a CPA firm showed up in their drab suits and read every piece of paper we'd filed since the last time they'd been there. When they found infractions, they were always small and easily fixable; Mark's work was above reproach, his books so meticulous that the Department of Education actually had asked him to be on a panel with the compliance auditors and to speak to other private-school business managers about the audit process. Despite his sometimes-questionable demeanor, believe it or not, Mark was actually regarded as an expert on private-school regulations and compliance at that time. As far as I was concerned, that was nothing but good news for all of us—and enough reason to overlook his personality flaws.

As part of each year's process, I gave the auditors tours of our schools so they could see what we actually did and how we made use of the purchases that they scrutinized on paper. I was happy to oblige; more time in the programs and less time sitting in the conference room answering their questions about the division of bookkeeping responsibilities and check authorization procedures seemed like a better proposition to me. I wasn't an accountant; I was an educator. And all that was the furthest thing from education I could think of.

So, there I was, at our old Somerset school, playing tour guide to six auditors—one team leader, whom I recognized from the previous year, and five new CPAs who all seemed inexplicably pleased with this assignment. Dave had decided to come along as well, along with a couple of people from the accounting office who hadn't seen the place before.

The more, the merrier, I thought as I led the group down the first hallway and wondered how I could make the tour last all day.

"Over here, you'll see our gymnasium," I told them, flourishing my arm toward the doorway like a game-show hostess announcing their big prize. They nodded and wrote down some notes. "Right now," I went on, "you can see one of our ninth-grade classes in there playing volleyball." I smiled at them brightly; they stared expressionlessly back at me. "The kids seem to really enjoy physical education and we think that having this sort of exercise break in their day is an excellent way to keep them focused on learning when they're in the classroom."

No response. I cleared my throat.

"Well," I said. "How about we go on and see those classrooms now?"

As we walked around the hallways, I let Dave take the lead for a while. He chitchatted with the auditors and gave them the background of our organization. "We founded the schools in 1986," he began, taking on the authoritative tone that those of use who worked with him knew well. Whenever he expounded on something—and I mean anything, from educational theory to the price of eggs—he switched on the charisma and turned into Dr. Dave, the Most Knowledgeable Man Alive. Most of the time, he sounded very convincing.

"We started with two schools," he went on, hands behind his back as he strolled along and addressed his audience. "Our mission was to provide the best educational services for New Jersey's disabled and special-needs kids—kids whose intellectual or physical differences kept them from fulfilling the requirements of a 'regular' education in a 'normal' classroom. Recognizing that students like these needed a different approach when it came to learning, Ellyn and I decided to open our own schools where we could offer specialized curricula that revolved around not just scholastic learning but behavioral, social, vocational and career training as well."

As Dave went on walking and talking, I thought back on those early days of New Road, which had been called High Road back then. We'd really shared a vision back then, before there'd been as much of a split between the central office and the schools. Together, we'd put a lot of sweat equity into the organization; we'd even funded our first school out of our own pockets, putting up our houses as collateral for bank lines of credit.

"By the year 2000," he was saying as we stopped outside a closed classroom door, "New Road was operating four schools in New Jersey—in Toms River, East Brunswick, Bergen County, and this one in Somerset. By that time we'd also branched out to other states, with one school each in Connecticut and Maryland. Right now, we're moving two of our schools into brand-new, state-of-the-art facilities in New Jersey, one in Parlin and one right here in Somerset."

Compared to what we'd started with, it was almost hard to believe that these new schools were really happening. One would have been inspiring; two new facilities fully equipped with every imaginable program for our students was indeed a feat.

"These are really going to be fantastic," Dave continued, and I nodded in agreement. "We've improved the layouts and functioning of our classrooms to encourage greater student independence, we've enhanced technological education, and we're making some major additions to our vocational training programs as well. Ellyn, that's more your area. Would you like to say a few words about it?"

I was leaning on the wall, listening to him, but stood up straight now and cleared my throat. "Well," I said, looking around at the glassy-eyed group, "in Somerset, for example, we'll still have all the work-training programs we have now—commercial arts, construction, cosmetology, food services, hospitality, natural sciences, information technology and premedical sciences. Students will attend courses in these subjects twice a week. In addition, we're building new career-training facilities, including actual working labs where the kids can learn the skills to become ophthalmological, dental or pharmaceutical assistants, and we're updating some of our other programs as well, like computer repair and home cable installation. Our students will graduate with advanced training and nationally recognized certificates that will allow them to compete in the workplace. In short, we're looking to create more of a career college atmosphere than a high school—the only one of its kind in the state and probably the country."

I finished with a big smile and flushed cheeks; the stuff we were doing in these schools was so thrilling to me, just thinking about it was exhilarating. Around me, though, there was no such reaction. In fact, it was so silent, I swore I could have heard crickets chirp. I waited for someone to ask me when we were going to break for lunch, or some other question that would verify just how uninterested they were. To say the least, I was a little disappointed.

"These are really revolutionary ideas we're working with here," I went on anyway, determined to get my point across whether they wanted to hear it or not. "No other school in the state can boast that level of job training for the population we serve. And it just goes to show how in touch we are with our students and their families—many of these ideas came from the parents themselves, who came to me asking for more opportunities for their children." I shrugged and smiled, a reflexive gesture that I repeated often when I spoke. "I guess you could say that they asked and we delivered."

Again there was some note scribbling, but that was about it. Usually, when I told people about my plans for the new Somerset school, they were amazed, and rightly so. Those were some awesome programs we were building. Your average vocational school for learning-disabled young adults taught trades such as food service and auto mechanics—which were fine for many people, and nothing to laugh at in the least. We had those programs as well, and we'd helped many, many young people prepare for jobs that they otherwise may never have considered.

However, there were some students for whom those programs were not enough. Students who wanted and needed to go further. And it was my mission to help them go as far as they could.

The work I did toward that end usually impressed people—and well it should have. We would be doing amazing things in those new schools, and most of it was based on my ideas. Of course, I've never been one to brag, but still, I was sometimes called selfless, a visionary, a saint for the work that I did. I wouldn't have said that I was any of those things, but I was modest; I just knew that I had a gift for helping kids who needed it and the ability—as well as the *responsibility*—to make things happen.

But not here, apparently. The auditors seemed unaffected by

anything I'd said, unimpressed by my organization's incredible achievements. I understood; it wasn't their role to be interested in our programs or our achievements. They were just there to check the books and records. Still, it hurt a little. I wanted the whole world to know how great New Road was and how many lives it had changed, and this group's apparent lack of admiration disappointed me. I loved my schools, I loved my students, and I wanted everyone else to love them, too. I guessed that to some people, all the good work we did just didn't mean a lot.

"Well," Dave said loudly at the front of the group, clapping his hands together once sharply to bring the group's attention back to him, "why don't we see what's going on in Mrs. Pat's science class? She's one of my favorite teachers—I'm sure she's up to something great!"

As he swung open the classroom door and ushered the auditors in, I leaned back against the wall again and closed my eyes, fearing that I was making a fool out of myself in front of these people. They didn't want rah-rah pep talks and company advertisements; they wanted papers and documents. They didn't want to be in the schools except to count our inventory of books, computers and supplies. I knew this; I just wished that they could open their hearts and minds up for five minutes and appreciate the miracle that was happening around them.

"Dr. Lerner, are you okay?"

I snapped my eyes open. I'd thought I was alone in the hallway, but there was Pamela Hall, New Road's controller, standing in front of me. She'd been working at New Road for a little over a year by that point; she was young and cute, a little anxious most of the time, I'd noticed, but on the whole pretty harmless. At the office she mostly kept to herself and, I assumed, did her job. Mark was her manager, so that was his area. I didn't make a point of checking up on employees who had their own higher-ups to report to.

"Pamela," I said to her with a smile, and reached out to squeeze her arm. "I'm so glad you wanted to come on the tour today. I think it's so important for everyone in the company to see the schools at least once. You really have to be here to get the feel of what we're all working for. And please, call me Ellyn."

"Uh, yeah," she said, looking up and down the hallway nervously. "Looks like a great place...if you like kids." She looked back at me for a moment in silence, then added quietly, "I can tell how much it all means to you."

I nodded. "It does, it means a lot," I told her. "Do you have any children?"

She laughed. "God, no, I hate them," she said abruptly. "I love dogs, though. My beagle and my husband are enough for me."

Though I was a little taken aback at her answer—disliking kids and working for a school was kind of like a vegetarian getting a job at a meat-packing plant—I smiled at her again anyway, hoping that this tour would at least give her an appreciation for what our company did.

"So, did you, like, um, go to college for this?" she asked.

"Sort of," I told her. "I was an education major, then I got a master's in remedial reading. Before this, I worked for another school where I taught kids with learning disabilities how to read."

"And that's what made you want to open your own school?"

I thought about it for a moment. "Yes, more or less," I said, which was accurate, but the simplified version. The work I'd done at that school had been groundbreaking—most notably my program to teach children how to read using sign language. These kids were not hearing impaired; they were severely dyslexic. They had trouble learning and retaining letters, words and sentences.

The issue first became apparent to me while working with a seven-year-old girl who just wasn't grasping the alphabet through traditional teaching methods. She was able to trace or write a letter, but once she was done, she just couldn't reiterate what it was. At the time, I wasn't sure how to better assist her, but as always, I knew there had to be a way. So, I did some research—not into other existing teaching methods that might have helped this girl but into the nature of her neurological disability. I didn't want to paste another cookie-cutter approach on her. Those didn't work for her. She needed something new, something that catered to her particular set of challenges.

I was an innovator, after all. I created paths; I didn't follow them. And I was going to help this girl—and other students like her—find hers.

I decided to tackle the problem from a neurological perspective—that is, to understand how the brain of a dyslexic student worked, in order to see what it needed in order to learn most effectively. Every person, regardless of ability, has two hemispheres in their brain, the right and the left, and each is responsible for a different set of skills. For example, your "left brain" controls your ability to write, speak, read, talk, listen and follow directions. Your "right brain" aids you with comprehension of spatial relationships, math, color sensitivity, artistic ability, emotions and the processing of images.

In a person who is dyslexic, there is a deficit in one side of the brain that affects how they experience, process and retain information from the world around them. What is known as a *right hemisphere lesioned dyslexic* who has problems with imagery would not be able to learn the alphabet using pictures of letters. They might, however, respond well to a reading program that focused on spelling rules and phonics.

The problem there was that at the time, many educational assessments were based upon certain standardized methods of teaching, i.e., a standardized test that was given to all students regardless of their particular neurological impairments. A severely dyslexic student is bound to do poorly on a traditional test that offers him or her only visual or pictorial cues.

So, where did that leave me and my seven-year-old student? To her, letters were little more than abstract symbols. I watched her day after day, tracing A, B and C with her pencil, knowing that she had no idea what they meant. She would even mouth the sounds of each letter as she wrote them, and still she would not remember them as soon as she put the pencil down.

So, what if, I thought, she had a more tangible cue to help her remember? Something that would work *with* the way her brain functioned instead of against it?

I knew some sign language, and I immediately thought of it as a solution. Imagery didn't work; teaching her orally didn't work. I'd had her glue sand to letter forms or trace them into surfaces covered in fur to make it more tactile. I'd made three-foot letters out of tape on the floor and had her walk around their outlines. Still, she showed no consistent pattern of recognition of their names.

Then, one day, it occurred to me: what about a *manual sign?* Something that she could perform again and again, something that would stay with her? Sign language seemed like it might be a good fit for her—it didn't rely on pictures, or speaking, or any of the modalities that had so far failed her. Maybe it was a long shot, but I had to try.

9

Creating a sign with a hand and looking at a picture of a hand making a sign use different functional sections of the brain. Creating the sign utilizes kinesthetic or haptic sensations while looking at the image is similar to visualizing an icon—a picture that stands for something else—which involves right-brain recognition. This is different from visualizing a symbol or a letter, which involves the left brain.

By using sign language with this student, I would be offering her a new pathway to the typical sound-symbol association teaching: visual symbol (the letter) to visual picture (the picture of the hand making the sign) to kinesthetic sensation (the formulation of the hand sign) to verbal response. My technique, although seemingly longer and more complex than any traditional method, would have the effect of taking a completely left-brain function (sound-symbol) and crossing it with two right-brain intermediaries (kinesthesia and pictorial identification).

So, I started teaching this girl the signs for the letters. I would show her the letter on paper, read it to her, then teach her the sign, associating all three approaches. Some days, she seemed to be really getting it; others, she was back to square one. But, she had more good days than bad, and in time, over months of trial and error, it appeared that she understood. She was learning. It was like a miracle—one I'd had a hand in creating.

In time, my student could identify almost the entire alphabet and over the course of seven months learned over 300 sight words through this method. She even learned phonemic awareness and, ultimately, sound blending for new words. When she could read short stories on a low, second-grade proficiency as well, I noticed that when she read aloud and came across a word that she wasn't quite sure of, she made the signs of the letters under her desk to retrieve or sound out the word. This was an incredible breakthrough.

I knew that I was onto something great. I demonstrated the technique to other teachers, and in trying it with other students we found that it worked for an aphasic subset of dyslexic students—which meant that my personalized approach and my belief in treating each person as an individual with unique abilities worked. I'd come up with a truly innovative—and, more importantly, truly effective—new method of teaching. It would become my hallmark, the base from which I really launched my educational career.

In time, I developed this right-brain reading method into a full-fledged program with a procedural manual and workbooks. Once it got dispersed out into the education community at large, I became sort of famous for it; I was featured in newspapers, traveled around the country giving presentations on the method and wrote an article about it that was published in *The Learning Consultant Journal*.

Strangely, the people who'd run the school for which I worked hadn't been too impressed by any of that; they would have preferred that I stick to more traditional methods of teaching. At that point, it had been obvious that if I ever wanted to make a difference in this world for people with learning disabilities, I had to strike out on my own, had to have my own facilities and population with which to work. I was dedicated to knowledge, to researching pedagogical approaches to all sorts of disabilities, and so incredibly enthusiastic about experi menting, innovating and creating new programs for students with low-incidence disabilities. I was also a determined workaholic who simply could not be stopped once I set my mind on something, and if the people at that school weren't going to let me do what I wanted, I was going to get it done on my own.

"I had a dream," I told Pamela, "of reforming not just specialized education but public schools as well. I thought that by making an impact in this field, I could help redefine how special ed kids are treated in typical schools."

"That's cool," she said, nodding her head slowly. Her nerves seemed to have calmed down a bit. I didn't know a whole lot about Pamela at the time, and had always wondered why she'd seemed so shaky. Several weeks earlier, it had occurred to me that maybe she had a drug or alcohol problem, and I'd considered talking to her about our employee-assistance program. But then I hadn't done it; whatever her problem, it really hadn't been affecting her work that I'd known of, and I just hadn't wanted to jump to conclusions or pry too deep. She was a new employee. I had told myself just to wait and see.

When she didn't say anything else, I shrugged and smiled again, my stand-by reflex. "It's hard to want to help others but not be able to," I told her, "and to work for a boss who doesn't understand you."

She laughed at that. "I know how *that* feels," she said, and I caught a note of what sounded like anger or sarcasm in her voice.

"Oh, yeah?" I replied, happy that we were making conversation. I even felt a little bad that I hadn't made more of an effort to get to know her before this. "Had a bad experience at another job or something?"

She looked at me and didn't say anything. Her eyes were starting to appear a little glassy, a little glazed over, and again I vaguely wondered if she was on some sort of drug, or maybe a medication. In my mind, I shuffled for the name of the employee-assistance program, tried to remember where we kept our stash of pamphlets about it. Maybe it was time to finally give her one.

Two

By four that afternoon, I was back at the office with my ear pressed up against the conference room door, trying to hear what was going down inside. So far, it had just been a lot of mumbling—none of the yelling and crying I had feared and almost expected.

"Ellyn?" Dave asked from down the hall, pausing on his way to the copier, a sheaf of papers on his hands. "What on earth are you doing?"

"Shh!" I told him as I tiptoed away from the door, a finger to my lips. "Pamela's in there with the auditors," I said. "I saw her coming out of Mark's office before going in, and it looked like she'd been crying."

Dave sighed. "Again?"

I nodded. It certainly hadn't been the first time I'd seen Pamela upset after a confrontation with a coworker. Every time Mark had questioned her work, it had seemed, she'd had a meltdown. Their interactions had been largely volatile. "I'm just a little afraid that she's going to take it out on the auditors."

"Don't trust her?" he asked me, laughing a little.

I grimaced. "Do you?" I asked back, sincerely wondering if he did, hoping that all the reservations I had about the girl were unfounded.

Dave paused for a moment, just long enough to show that he had to consider his answer. "Well," he offered, "I don't *not* trust her. Honestly, I don't know her well enough to say either way."

I looked back toward the conference room door, wishing I could hear more of what they were saying in there. "I don't, either," I told him. "And that's what makes me so nervous."

I went back into my office then and tried to get some of my own paperwork done. I tried to keep my mind off of the audit, but it was difficult. Based on the conversation I'd had with Pamela Hall earlier that day, I found myself suddenly wary of her, and I wondered just how well

13

she could handle this sort of pressure. This was only her second time going through an audit with us, and her first time with such a big role in it; the previous year, she'd been new to the company and had mostly just observed the process. Given what I'd seen of her anxious nature since then, I was afraid that the stress just might make her crack.

———

"Oh, yes, I have tons of experience with auditing!" Pamela told the group inside the conference room—proving me, though I didn't know it at the time, completely wrong. In front of them, she was confident, poised and knowledgeable, everything she didn't seem to be normally around the rest of us in the office. "I was in charge of the auditing periods at my two previous jobs, and I'm really happy to be stepping into the same role here."

"How long have you worked at New Road?" one of the auditors asked, looking up from the paperwork he was inspecting. Older and slightly balding, he sported a thin mustache and tired eyes that looked like they'd read about a million boring spreadsheets and then some.

"Just over a year," Pamela responded cheerily. "And I love it here!"

Now, had I been there—or had I at least still had my ear to the door—I probably would have started laughing at that point. Pamela Hall, in love with New Road? That would have been news to me. She always walked around the office with a sour look on her face, and I rarely heard her say anything that was too friendly or even very positive; she seemed miserable a lot of the time and certainly nothing about her work duties seemed to cheer her up. She was definitely laying it on thick for the auditors.

"And what do you do here on a day-to-day basis?" asked another auditor—a woman, middle-aged, wearing a light-pink suit. She didn't bother to take her eyes off of the accounting log before her.

"Well, a big part of my job has been to tighten up the company's internal controls," Pamela replied. "I've been working on making sure that all our policies and procedures when it comes to purchasing are updated, in place and being followed."

"Such as?" the first auditor asked, looking at Pamela over the top of his reading glasses.

She cleared her throat and took a moment, but then went on without faltering. "Such as updating our actual purchase order forms, revising the rules on who gets to make purchases and the guidelines for purchasing, creating a hierarchy for who gets to approve the orders—that sort of thing."

A silence filled the room except for the sound of flipping pages as the audit team made their way through our records. Pamela sat at the head of the table, her hands folded, and looked down the line at each of them.

"We have a lot of good controls already in place," she added, feeling a little bold thanks to her apparent success with these people. "I'm just making sure that they're the best they can be. That New Road is the best that it can be."

After a few days of this, Pamela's smile seemed to fade a little, and her impatience with the audit process began to show through, though I have to admit that she continued to hold it together pretty well in front of the audit team. Though she was as snappy as usual with her coworkers, she was polite and efficient with the auditors, supplying them with any of the information they needed and making sure that the rest of the accounting and bookkeeping staff did the same. Of course, she did have Mark supervising her, so the weight of the audit didn't fall completely on her shoulders, but she did have her stake in the matter and she played it out well. After she'd made it through almost five weeks of this scrutiny, I had to admit that maybe my initial doubts about her had been for nothing.

As was customary toward the last days of the audit, Mark, Dave and I were all called into the conference room, first alone and then together, to be grilled by the auditors regarding New Road's accounting practices. They wanted to hear that we were all on the same page, I figured, when it came to where, when and how our money was spent. As usual, they found little that did not please them.

"Your invoicing is very organized," one of them said to me during my interview. "The itemization on them is phenomenal. Who came up with that idea?"

"Well, I did, sort of," I replied, giving them the short answer. The long answer was that ten years earlier, the Department of Education's

Office of Fiscal Accountability had been doing a financial audit of New Road, and their representative had told me to start itemizing everything we purchased into component parts. That meant that if we bought, for example, some playground equipment, we shouldn't just list it as a "jungle gym" on the invoice—we should break it down into a swing set for $1,000, a slide for $500 and so on.

"It was on the recommendation of a Department of Ed auditor," I added, just to be clear on it.

They looked at me blankly—their usual expression. Nothing about this demeanor alarmed me.

"The New Jersey Department of Education told you to do this?" one of them asked.

I nodded. "Yes. The representative's name was Ms. Ming. She actually said that our invoices were sloppy because they weren't itemized, and advised us to start doing so right away. I ran it by our accountants and auditors at the time, and they said it was fine. They even said I should take it a step further and itemize any labor that each purchase required."

"So, how would you classify these purchases, then?" another auditor asked—the older gentleman who had seemed so interested in Pamela back on the first day of the audit. "As expense items or capital items?"

"Well, in accordance with the state regulations, if they were under two thousand dollars, they would be expenses. Anything over that amount, of course, would be capitalized. But the auditors we had at that time told me that any item could be classified as either expense or capital depending on its use." I shrugged and smiled. "I'm not an accountant. I let Mark and his people handle all that."

The auditor nodded, his eyebrows lowered as he perused a spreadsheet he held in his hand. "And so you implemented these suggestions from...Ms. Ming?"

"Of course," I said. "I always follow the recommendations of the state authorities. They're our number-one client." I smiled at him, and he just nodded back. My charm, as usual, was completely lost on these people. "We developed a policy requiring any large-scale purchases to be itemized into their component parts, and we began keeping records of how we used the things we bought, when they were repaired, any wear or damage and so on. Oh, we also set an approval threshold for purchasing."

"And what is that threshold?" asked one of the younger auditors, who by now had taken on the dour demeanor of his colleagues. Gone was his first-day enthusiasm and excitement, poor thing. I almost felt bad for him.

"Currently, it's two thousand dollars," I told them. "It's been that way for a while. Basically, we do this to encourage our employees to make reasonable and cost-effective purchasing decisions. To really look at what they're spending and what they're getting for it. It also helps them match up each option on a piece of equipment ordered with each item that was actually received."

The older auditor spoke up again. "So you're saying that you don't allow anyone to make purchases over two thousand dollars?"

I shook my head. "No, no. They can purchase items over that amount. They just have to itemize them on the invoices so that their component parts stay beneath that threshold. That's what Ms. Ming told me to do, and it was approved by our accountants and auditors. And by *your* auditors, too—we've been doing it for years, and your firm has signed off on it at every audit."

The auditors finally looked up from their papers but not at me—instead, they eyed each other. As if through some sort of hive-mind telepathy, they seemed to come to a consensus that this practice was just fine by them; they nodded at each other, then went back to their papers.

"Dr. Lerner, thank you for your time," said the older gentleman. "Would you please tell Dave that we are ready to speak with him?"

After seeing the auditors out on their last day, I said a silent prayer of thanks that they were out of our hair for another year and then headed straight to Mark's office to talk to him about fourth-quarter spending. I hadn't wanted to bother him with it during the audit, knowing how much work he'd already had to do, but now that it was over with I needed to get him onboard. It was only April but before we knew it, we'd be planning our projects for 2004—and paying for them with what was left of our 2003 budget. I had to make sure that all the controls for that were in place and ready to go.

His office door was open, but hearing voices inside, I stopped in the hallway, pausing for a moment just out of sight. From inside, I heard the familiar whine of Mark's angry voice and the accompanying high treble of Pamela trying to defend herself. They were arguing again. The sound of it was, unfortunately, familiar to me.

"God damn it, Pamela, you were supposed to have this done *months* ago," Mark shouted, and I could hear him slamming a book onto his desk. "You've been here for more than a year. You couldn't find a *few* minutes *somewhere* to get up to speed on the regulations?"

I sighed and put a hand up to my forehead. *This again*, I thought, a feeling of dread creeping into my stomach. How many times had Mark complained to me that Pamela just was not grasping the state regulations under which New Road operated? As controller, knowing those rules was a very, very important part of her job; she should have memorized them by then, been able to recite them backwards and forwards. If she didn't know them, how had she gone through the audit with so much confidence? Perhaps, I thought, she hadn't done as great a job as I'd thought after all.

"I gave you an outline of the regulations when I hired you," Mark went on, his voice full of venom. "I didn't even make you read the entire book. How much easier can I make it for you? Did you even read what I gave you?"

"Yes, I read it," Pamela said, obviously through clenched teeth. "It's a lot of information to take in all at once."

Mark sighed, loudly and dramatically. "Well, what can I do, Pamela? How can I *make* you remember? Do I have to give you pop quizzes like you're in fifth grade? Hold your hand? Give you a cookie every time you do something right?" He slammed his hand down on the desk, rattling a cup of pens so badly that it fell to the floor. "Listen, you're a good accountant, Pamela, but this is a regulated business. You have to understand compliance. Do you know what the fuck this business does?"

"I—" Pamela began, but Mark would not let her get in another word.

"I'll fire your ass, Pamela," he said. "And then maybe I can hire someone who *can* do this job." There was a moment of very uncomfortable silence, and then he added, "Out. Get out of my office. Get out of my sight."

Before I even thought to move out of the way, Pamela Hall came barreling out of Mark's office, a notebook labeled REGULATIONS clutched to her chest. Jumping in surprise when she saw me standing there, she stopped for a moment and gave me an icy look, as if I had been the one threatening to can her. Then, without a word, she stomped past me, went into her own office and slammed the door.

Inside, Mark was pacing behind his desk and wiping sweat from his brow.

"You've gotta lighten up on her," I told him quietly, closing the door behind me. "Really, Mark, do you have to *yell* so much?"

"Well, what would you do, huh?" he shouted at me, whipping his hand out into the air in exasperation. "She's a deer in headlights all the time. She doesn't seem to know all the regulations we're working with yet, and she doesn't ask me for help when she needs it. If I question how she did something, she just gives me a blank stare."

"Mark, you—" I began, but then he cut me off, too, like he did to everyone when he wanted to get his point across.

"I mean, she misclassified over twenty non-certified assistants as classroom teachers in our records for the audit. Can you blame me for being so mad?"

I sighed then, too, and sat down in one of the chairs in front of his desk. "Is that why she came out of your office upset before going in with the auditors?"

He threw his hands in the air once again. "Yes, but what was I supposed to do? She fucked up. I had to let her know. Sorry if my timing wasn't perfect."

I motioned for him to sit down, too. "Mark, you're a fantastic CFO and a wonderful accountant," I told him, "but you're terrible with people. There are better ways to deal with employees who aren't up to snuff."

He looked at me for a moment then pulled out his chair and dropped down into it. Putting his hands behind his head, he leaned back and spun around, blowing out a long breath. When he faced me again, he smiled, but there was no joy in it. Just anger, frustration, disgust—all the emotions, I imagined, he felt when he had to deal with Pamela. Or anyone, for that matter. When it came to people, Mark just didn't have it in him.

"Well, we can't all be like you, Ellyn," he said.

I smiled and shrugged. At the moment, there was nothing else I could do.

Three

By March 2004, I'd been in our new Somerset facility dozens of times but still, when I walked through its doors on a Tuesday afternoon with a group of teachers and staff in tow, it was like I was seeing it for the first time all over again. I had already gotten used to the place, had grown accustomed to its high ceilings, its huge windows, the mingled smells of sawdust and sheetrock. Through my staff's fresh eyes, I was again able to see the promise of success that hung in the new school's air.

The lobby was still under construction but the reception desk was in place, as was the wall where we would feature photos of school events and employees and students of the month. To the left, there was nothing but ladders, drop cloths and paint buckets where, soon, there would be rows of lockers and classrooms. To the right lay what would become our administrative area, ten offices and a conference room from which my staff and I would run the entire production.

"There's not a *whole* lot to look at yet," I told the group as we paused in the entryway. Each of them looked up and around at the high ceiling, the huge windows, with expressions of curiosity and excitement on their faces. I smiled at their reactions, so happy that I had brought them here—even though I'd had to give their students a half-day to do it. "But if you can use your imaginations a little, I'm sure you'll see just how incredible this place is going to be."

For weeks, I'd been splitting my days between Somerset, the new school in Parlin and, when I had to, our main office. I had taken a special interest in the construction of our new classrooms and career labs and wanted to make sure that the contractors were creating everything to my specifications, that all the details, down to the last nut and bolt, would be perfect. So far, everything was. The whole project was going exactly as I wanted it to, and it was a pleasure to watch it all happen day by day.

"Let's go through here first," I told the group, making my way into the area to the left of the reception desk. "This is going to be a café of sorts, a restaurant where students and staff can eat. We'll have tables and booths, and everything will be prepared by students in our kitchen—which is right back here, if you'll follow me."

I led them into the food preparation area—a real, working kitchen that would rival any large restaurant's facilities.

"Wow," said Pat Culp, one of our longtime career counselors. She was one of the kids' favorites, a really great member of our team with a talent for helping even the toughest cases. Running her hand along one of the stainless-steel countertops, she let out a low whistle. "This place is no joke!"

Everyone laughed at that, including me. "You're absolutely right," I told her. "It's not. Our students will *really* be learning how to work in a food service environment here, from dish washing to deep frying to working the counter to serving in our fine-dining restaurant. Everything they would need to get a job in the restaurant industry after they graduate."

Ms. Culp nodded appreciatively as she turned a sink's faucet on and off. No water yet—not while construction was still going on. Still, she and everyone else seemed very impressed, and of course that pleased me to no end. I was proud of the kitchen and café—but even more so of the other career-training programs we were putting in place. I couldn't wait to show them the rest of the facility.

"Let's keep moving," I told the group, moving toward the door. "There's a lot more to see, and I don't want to keep you here all night!"

En route to the other career-training labs, I took the staff on a pass through the fitness center, stopping to let them envision the Precor and Curves exercise machines that would soon be arriving. Not content to have just a regular old high-ceilinged, basketball-court-style gym like any other school, we sought to meet our students' physical fitness needs through more modern means; they'd told me they wanted a real fitness center to work out in, like they'd go to out in the community, and that was just what I was going to give them.

With the group behind me, I moved out into the hallway again and down toward the other new programs that were still being built. First was the med-tech and pharmacology labs, where students would learn first aid skills and the basics of medication administration—topics that could prepare them to work as EMTs, pharmacy assistants or even medical office staff. Next was the dental lab, a room that was outfitted with three actual dental-office chairs where students would learn how to take X-rays, do teeth impressions, tray sterilization and preparations, and all the standard tasks that any assistant in a dentist's practice might perform.

"And now," I told the group as we arrived at one of my favorite rooms in the building, "get ready for something *really* impressive."

Leading the group into the eye lab—one of the only setups that was almost entirely finished at that point—I couldn't help but feel a swell of pride in my chest, a flush of excitement in my cheeks. This one really had been my baby, a project that had been mine from its inception, and seeing it almost up and running was beyond words. There was a small lobby of sorts where students could learn how to run a retail frame-selection store in any ophthalmological practice, and then a back room where we had real, working eye exam machines and lens-grinding equipment, prescription-testing equipment and everything they needed to prepare them for careers as ophthalmology assistants. This was not just any ordinary career-training center; this was several steps above and beyond what any other school was offering at the time.

"Dr. Lerner," said Marcelle Roberts as the rest of the group walked around the lab, touching the machines and reading the standard, lettered eye exam charts on the walls. "This is incredible. I can't believe we're going to have something so…so…state of the art! But one question," she added, coming in a little closer, her voice lowering. "How are we *paying* for all of this?"

I smiled at her. Mrs. Roberts, being one of only a few administrators with authorization to make large purchases of supplies and equipment for the school, would ask a question like that—and rightly so, I thought. I'd given her that authorization because over the years she had shown me that she understood our "most bang for the buck" strategy. She'd always been a wise purchaser and I was glad to see that even here, she was putting that talent to use.

"Well, everything is coming out of this year's budget," I told her as I watched the others mill about. "All this, the other labs, the fitness center, the kitchen supplies—everything we need for here and the new building in Parlin as well."

She lowered her eyebrows. "Is that per the state regulations?" she asked, smiling a little nervously. "I thought they liked things to be bought in an installment-sale manner, especially if they're being bought ahead of time, before they'll be put into use."

I looked at Mrs. Roberts for a moment, impressed by her thorough understanding of the purchasing policies and procedures under which we operated. *If only* all *our staff had such a handle on it*, I thought ruefully, an image of Pamela Hall's scowling face floating through my mind.

I smiled and shrugged. "The way I see it," I explained, "we're buying the equipment this year, so it has to come out of this year's budget. Rather than capitalizing it and spreading the cost out over, say, the next five years, I'd rather just pay for it all now and not put the school in any unnecessary debt—especially since our costs will rise next year, thanks to the mortgage payments on this new building. They'll be considerably higher than this year's rent on the building you're in now."

Mrs. Roberts nodded. It did make sense; she couldn't deny that. What good would it do to put New Road in debt to pay for the massive amount of equipment that we needed right away? If we did it the long way, we'd have to take out loans from a bank and spread out the repayments (including an added ten-percent financing charge) over five years. Of course, the Department of Education would say that was all "allowable" expenses, but I just thought it was a waste. If we had the money in our current budget, then why not use it instead of sending it back to the state at the end of the year and putting ourselves in major debt to boot?

All we had to do to make this plan work was avoid capitalizing by keeping each purchase under $2,000, the state's limit on expensed equipment and supplies, and we were already doing that with our itemized invoicing. When building out this new school and the other one in Parlin, I'd specifically told everyone who ordered equipment to itemize all component parts ordered and to make sure that no component over $2,000 was purchased. I'd just reviewed that practice with our financial auditors, and they had given it the A-okay. They'd also said that if we kept our purchases under $2,000 per item, we wouldn't build up assets on our balance sheet, and in their opinion, fewer assets was safer for us. Given all that, it seemed to me like what we were doing here was in the clear as long as no individual item exceeded the Department of Education threshold.

What it came down to, I suppose, is that there was nothing in the regulations that said we couldn't expense large-scale purchases instead of capitalizing them—though, I knew, there was nothing saying that we *could*, either. The rule just said to follow the IRS and Generally Accepted Accounting Principles (GAAP) and to capitalize all fixed assets in excess of $2,000. Like so many IRS codes, what constituted a "fixed asset" and what got capitalized versus expensed was rather a gray area, a judgment call that I felt justified in making. According to the IRS rules, startup costs were not fixed assets, and that was what I considered all the money we spent on new equipment for our new schools to be: startup costs. The costs of starting up new facilities. It makes sense. It did to me at the time, anyway, and so I just went with it.

In retrospect, I guess that maybe I was using my own interpretation of the code to the school's advantage. But it wasn't a crime, it wasn't a violation—hell, it wasn't even a big deal. No one was getting any undue benefit out of it. If anything, I was saving the school money, and it seemed to me that the state would undoubtedly like that in the long run. Besides, it was something I'd done for years, and no one—no state inspectors, no private auditors and none of our accountants or controllers—had ever said one negative word about it.

"Listen, the state wants us to buy the equipment and then put it into use immediately," I tried explaining to Mrs. Roberts, to make the situation clearer. "But we just can't do that in this situation. We need the equipment ahead of time to—" I gestured around us, at the machines, the tables and chairs, the posters, the cabinets, the books. "We need all this now, so it's all ready when the kids finally get here. How can we wait to buy it until the moment when we need it? That just isn't practical, I'm sorry to say."

Mrs. Roberts silently eyed me in a way that I didn't entirely enjoy.

"We're not doing anything wrong," I told her, putting a hand on her shoulder. I didn't want her to lose confidence in the school, in me or in our mission. I wanted her to be as excited as I was about this new facility and all the amazing opportunities it would offer our students.

"Listen, just don't worry about it right now, okay? Just tell the vendors that for accounting purposes, you need complete itemization of all component parts that you are ordering. We're not doing anything technically wrong. And if anything does come up to worry about, I'll take care of it. Worrying about the method is my job. Preparing our amazing kids for the best futures they can possibly have is yours. Okay? We have a deal on that?"

She smiled at me then and nodded, and I knew she was back with me. Mrs. Roberts had been with New Road for over a decade; she'd started out as a teacher assistant then become a teacher, a head teacher and now a program director, and I couldn't imagine not having her support. My relationships with my staff meant everything to me, and knowing that they did not have complete faith in either me or my work would have been devastating.

"Are we ready to move on?" I asked the group, throwing one last warm smile in Mrs. Roberts' direction. She smiled back, and I felt so much more at ease.

Four

L eaning back in my desk chair, sipping from a paper cup of luke-warm coffee, I stared out the window for a moment while I waited for one of my regional directors to call me back. A light snow fell from the sky, dusting the dump trucks and the contractors' pick-ups out in the lot. I hoped that they hadn't left any of our new equipment exposed to the elements.

Last thing we need right now is damaged equipment, I thought, imagining what a monumental hassle it would be to have to reorder things at this point. The invoicing alone would be a nightmare.

It was January 2004, just a few months before my entire world would be turned upside down, though I had no clue about it at the time. To me, it was just another Wednesday, another day I was tied to the main office in the not-yet-open Parlin school. Headset on my ears, I had been playing air traffic controller with my satellite staff all morning, calling each regional director in turn, asking for their weekly reports.

A buzz in my ear let me know that Karin was calling me back. Head of one of our out-of-state school regions, she was always busy, always a little hard to get a hold of. Sometimes, this irked me but in general, I thought it was good. At least she was out there working, not just sitting in her office playing principal.

"Karin," I said, clicking on the headset. "How's everything in Connecticut today?"

"Sunny and mild," she boomed back cheerily, forcing me to adjust my receiver's volume, "but there's a forecast for snow this afternoon. And how's everything with you? How are the new New Jersey schools coming?"

I smiled, so happy that my staff—even those who were not directly involved—took an interest in other areas of our organization, and especially in our flagship schools' expansion. "Going great, Karin," I told her. "Just a few months away from completing construction. We'll be ready to open long before September gets here."

"Great news, great news! So, what can I do for you today?"

And with that, we launched into the regular question-and-answer routine that I went through with each of my regional and school directors on a weekly basis. In order to effectively run New Road and keep it at the top of its game, I had to have my finger on the pulse of each region, and the best way to do that, I thought, was to stay involved with the people who ran them.

During these phone calls, I always wanted to know three things: how enrollment was going, the types of problems they were working on with their directors, and the types of issues that their directors were addressing with their teachers. Based on these, I would be able to determine leadership styles and abilities and if the schools were adhering to our unique, proprietary model of instruction, behavior and supervision. If they were, the ship was running a smooth course. If anything was awry, then we had to set a plan in place—what we called *interventions*—to fix it.

This week, Karin did have some troubles worth noting.

"I don't know what to do," she told me. "We're having some issues getting a couple of our newer teachers onboard. We've trained them on the model, we've offered them support, but they just don't seem to be picking it up as quickly as they need to." There was a pause, as though she were considering whether or not she wanted to say something else. "Ellyn, it just feels to me like they're being lazy," she finally added. "Like they don't want to do so much work."

And there it was, that word: *lazy*. One of my hot buttons, a descriptor I listened for whenever I talked to my regional directors. More often than not, when they described someone as *lazy*, it meant that they—the directors—were somehow not responding to their staff the way they should be, not offering them the support they needed or addressing their concerns in some manner. The problem, I'd found, was not actual laziness; it was just fear coupled with a breakdown in communication. Usually, teachers deemed "lazy" just did not have full faith that our model would bring about the results in student learning and behavior that we all required.

"They're not lazy," I told Karin. "They're just not on the same level as you yet. You have to look at the situation realistically, not just through the lens of our vision and standards. Yes, we want everyone to be just as gung ho as we are about New Road's mission and goals, but we have to give them time to get there. Everyone starts out on their own level, and they can only move forward one step at a time."

There was more silence, another pause while she thought about what I'd said. "Maybe we're throwing too much at them at once," she admitted. "But you wanted me to increase my accountability quotient, and aren't I holding them accountable?"

Each school and regional director's interventions with their staff were judged on their balance of empathy and accountability as well as their effectiveness in running our unique model of classroom structure. Karin always placed high on our empathy scale but low on accountability, so the interventions I did with her were devised primarily to increase the latter while keeping the former in check. Frequently, during our weekly phone calls, we reviewed her list of promises and ensured that she was meeting her requirements on both fronts.

"Yes," I replied to her, nodding my head, "but you can't hold them accountable for things that you haven't yet taught them or interventions that you haven't suggested. You have to call them into individual meetings, lay out your requests and then hold them accountable to completing those. You have to be specific. You can't make them accountable for—I don't know, being a great teacher. You *can* make them accountable for implementing the components of the model that you stress to them during the individual meetings, especially once they've promised to fulfill your request. Move them along at their own pace, with some gentle but very firm encouragement and explicit, agreed-upon interventions, and they'll get where they need to be."

"And if they don't," she said, sounding as though she was getting it, "then I'll question why they didn't fulfill their promises and agreements, and they will choose to straighten it out or not. Only at that point can I determine if they're a mismatch." She paused again, thinking, then added, "I have a lot more work to do with some of this staff before I make that determination."

It pleased me that she said all of this, because that idea was truly the heart of my business philosophy, the model on which I ran my schools: As a leader, you have to love your people—a phrase that I used quite frequently—and you have to show them that affinity by accepting them where they are and helping them become the highest vision of who they would like to be. Each interaction you have with them must build either their confidence or competency, and any intervention you propose must be aimed at building their greatness. The day you can no longer love your people, you have to let them go—for the good of both the organization and the employee.

Confident that Karin and I were on the same page with this issue, we went on to formulate a plan to remedy the situation. She agreed to talk to her directors—the ones who actually had the most contact with the teachers and were responsible for monitoring them—and have them step back the training to levels that were more comfortable for the teachers in question. She would do this that day, and call me the next day with an update.

Clicking the phone off, I went back to sipping my coffee, now cold, and looking out the window at the snowfall, wondering again about the equipment in those trucks.

Two phone calls and one more cup of coffee later, my administrative assistant, Kathy, poked her head in the door.

"Dr. Lerner?" she asked brightly, and I could tell she was in a playful mood—normally, she only called me by my first name. "Would you like to join us for lunch today?"

Looking over at her, I smiled and took off my headset. "Is it that time already?" I asked her, glancing down at my watch. Ten after noon. I couldn't believe the morning had gone so fast.

I wasn't hungry, but I thought about going into the lunchroom and spending some time with Kathy and the rest of them—Dave and Mark, Jill, Antoinette, maybe Pamela Hall if she felt like coming out of her office, the rest of the accounting staff and assistants. Sometimes, it was nice to be together with all of them, to feel like part of the team. Sometimes, though...

"I don't know," I told Kathy, shrugging my shoulders apologetically. "I just don't think I'm up to it today."

She gave me a look that told me she knew exactly how I felt. "Don't blame you," she said, her mood visibly deflating. "I don't know why I go, either. Don't you think it's kind of funny that we have such an amazing culture in our schools, that everyone there gets along so well, and here—"

"Here you can't even get people to be cordial to one another?"

She looked at me in silence for a moment, and I could tell she was exasperated by it—as was I. New Road's main office had long been a completely different animal from its school facilities. The latter ran on my "love your people" policy and encouraged everyone to truly do their best, to strive to achieve their goals and to rely on one another's help and encouragement to get there. At the office, it was more divide and conquer, more authoritarian: Orders were barked, deadlines were set without consultation or agreement between boss and subordinate, and, worst of all, lunchroom discussions, more often than not, devolved into grade-school mockery of fellow employees, whether they were present or not. It wasn't just mild joking around, either. I'm talking all out vitriol, stuff I wouldn't have said even to someone I hated.

And all of this, I'm sorry to say, was led by Dave and Mark. As the office figureheads, they set the tone for everyone else, and the atmosphere they created was definitely negative at times. I'm not saying that they did it willfully; they were just caustic, with acidic tongues and dry senses of humor, and did not understand that not everyone shared their delight in making fun of their subordinates. I tried explaining to both of them, time and again, that employees only laughed at their "jokes" because they were the bosses, and nobody wanted to go against the guys in charge. Whenever our employees told me how much they dreaded the daily lunch hour, I let Dave and Mark know, and asked them to tone it all down. But all my complaints fell on deaf ears, and the mockery continued.

Part of the problem was that I didn't have direct authority over Dave; he was my business partner, not my employee, so there was nothing I could do to ameliorate the situation on his side. Besides, it was so obvious that he didn't want to change. "I deliver only A-plus material," he told me once, waving away my complaint. "People need a little fun, and I'm in charge of giving it to them."

As for Mark, I was able to tone him down occasionally, but when it was just him and Dave in the office together for days on end, that harsh mockery came out in full force. Most of the time, I just gave up on the problem and remained thankful that neither of them had any presence or influence in the schools.

"Good luck," I told Kathy. "Feel free to come in here if you can't take it anymore."

She nodded, her face somber. "Probably see you in a few minutes, then."

Half an hour later, there was a knock on my office door.

Kathy, I thought, shaking my head sadly. *She held out longer than I thought she would.*

"Come in," I called, hanging up on the phone number I had been dialing—the last of my regional director calls for the day.

To my surprise, when the door opened, Dave walked in.

"Dave," I greeted him warmly, flashing back to the conversation I'd had with Kathy. I wondered if he'd just come from a good session of ridiculing his employees in the lunchroom—but then I felt a little guilty about it. Dave was a good friend to me, and invaluable to my own confidence and competence in running the company. Charming, benevolent, visionary and influential with New Road's external constituents, he was high-powered and brilliant, full of wisdom and substantive perspectives, especially when it came to the regulatory, political environment in which our organization operated. He had such great insight into the education field, I really couldn't have created or expanded New Road or our other schools without him. Maybe he could have been more patient with our employees or tried to appear as less of a dictator. But overall, he had far fewer bad qualities than outstanding ones, and I reminded myself that it was the latter on which I should focus.

"Ellyn," he replied, coming in and sitting down in front of my desk. "How are all the directors today?"

"No major issues," I replied, remembering that I still had my headset on. I reached up and disentangled it from my curly hair. "Enrollment is up overall," I added as I fought with the equipment, finally getting it off and tossing it onto the desk.

"That's great," Dave said, but his tone was off-handed, and he was looking out the window as he spoke to me. It was obvious there was something else on his mind.

"So, what's going on?" I asked him.

He looked back at me. "I'm thinking about retiring," he said plainly, as if we were discussing the weather. "Well, not really, fully retiring. I just don't want to be an owner of our schools anymore. I'd like to stay on as a consultant but not be involved with the ownership function. "

Well, you could've knocked me over with a feather. Dave wanted to leave New Road? That was craziness. I couldn't imagine him not working, and especially not working with me. What on earth would I do without him? He was my confidante, my source of strength. I *could* run the whole place but did I really want the burden of sole ownership?

Oh, God, don't tell me I'd have to be in the office every day without visiting the schools! I thought, some initial panic setting in.

Dave, sensing my trepidation, put his hands up to stop me. "Wait," he said, sitting forward in his chair. "I don't mean *today.* I don't even mean this semester. Probably sometime this year but definitely not without some planning. I've been thinking about it, and I could keep working as a consultant. I just no longer want to be an owner—only a founder."

I took a deep breath. I didn't want to imagine owning the entire operation without him, but I had to try to see his side of it. "Well, I have to say, I wasn't expecting that," I told him with a laugh. "So, tell me, what brought all of this on?"

"Well," he began, sitting back in his chair again, obviously relieved that I wasn't going to start an argument with him over it. "I just turned sixty-two. And I have grandchildren I'd like to spend some time with while I'm still young enough to play with them. Besides, after I had that last heart attack, I decided that I really don't want any more stress in my life, and let me tell you, Ellyn, fighting with you has been way too stressful."

And there it was. From the minute he'd said it, I'd known I somehow would be blamed for his decision. Yes, we argued a lot, but I hardly felt like I was the sole source of his tension. Though he claimed to hate stress, he often criticized or asked questions that would put anyone on the defensive, and then would fight with anyone who did defend themselves—almost like he enjoyed it. Like he *looked* for the stress.

As far as his health, his last heart attack had been eight years earlier, and he'd always feared another; he also had a growing problem with arthritis and back pain that made his hour-and-a-half commute to work more and more onerous every month. If he didn't want to drive that much anymore, I could understand it. Plus, his wife had just retired, and so if he had an opportunity to spend more time with her and their beautiful grandchildren, how could I blame him for wanting to take it? How could anyone?

"Now, as an alternative," he went on, shaking me out of my thoughts, "our shareholder agreement said that when either partner reaches the age of sixty-two, they can force the other to buy them out."

He stopped, and that one just hung there like a lead balloon. *Buy him out?* I thought. *With what money?* I had a life, too; I had my own financial situation to worry about. I wasn't doing poorly, but I had a mortgage, I had loans. I had obligations that would make a buyout— well, not something I really wanted to do just then. Dave had mentioned it numerous times before, but only in anger after a big fight, or at times when he'd felt insignificant as far as the schools were concerned. This was the first time he'd said it outside the context of stressful disagreement, and the first time that I was taking him seriously.

"Again," he said, holding up his hands once more. "Not something I want right this minute. I just—you know, Ellyn, neither of us has ever taken any profits from this place. Don't you think that it's time we did? Neither of us is getting any younger, and though I know you do, I *don't* want to reinvest every penny into this operation anymore. Our goals are different. And I'd like to start taking out some of the value that we've built."

And at that, I sat back, too, and I smiled. He was right. I was no spring chicken anymore. But, I had plenty of good years ahead of me, of that I was certain, lots of precious time that I planned to spend making New Road the best school system in the country. Retirement was not on my radar, but I could understand why it was on his: because he spent all his time here in this office. Because he wasn't as involved with the schools as I was. Because although he cared about New Road's impact and legacy, his day-to-day passion was not for people but for papers and numbers—all things that could easily be left behind.

In a way, I felt almost sorry for him because of that. But even more so, I understood why he wanted to be bought out, why he wanted more freedom, and why it would probably not hurt him as much as it would me when my day finally came.

"Well," I told him, feeling a little calmer. "I'm glad you told me about it now, and I know we'll work something out. You really don't have any retirement date in mind?"

He shrugged, holding his hands out in a questioning gesture. "Who knows?" he replied. "I'm in no hurry to actually retire. I'm more interested in the ownership issue."

I nodded. "Thanks for that, Dave," I said. "I really appreciate it. Let's keep talking about it, alright? Keep the lines open. Especially where the buyout's concerned. That's something we'll have to look into."

He nodded, too, and got up from his chair. He paused for a moment, looking out the window again, rubbing his chin with his hand as if thinking about something else again.

"Anything more you want to talk about?" I asked him, wishing that if there were, he'd just come out and say it.

He looked back at me and after a brief pause, he smiled, and I noticed that there was suddenly a lot more salt in his salt-and-pepper beard. Sometimes, I thought, he really did look like he was getting old. We'd been partners for so long, I didn't always notice it, but when I really stopped and looked... Well, the telltale signs were there.

"No," he said, "nothing else. Listen, I'll catch you later. Gonna go see what's going on in the lunchroom."

By six o'clock, I was way more than ready to head home. After my surprise meeting with Dave, I'd spent most of the afternoon on the phone again, finishing up my calls to the regional directors and following up on some other issues I'd been putting off. I'd wanted to get everything done so I could spend the rest of the week in the schools, and at the end of the day, I was worn out because of it.

Briefcase in hand, pocketbook slung over my shoulder and a stack of full, manila folders clutched in my free arm, I headed out into the lobby, steadying myself for the long trudge out to the car.

"Ellyn, Ellyn!" someone called from behind me, and I stopped in my tracks and sighed. I just wanted to go home. What was so important that someone had to chase me out to the lobby at the last minute?

I turned around slowly, wiping the exhausted expression off my face and reminding myself that I loved my people, that I had to be there for them when they needed me, and that I should be nice to whomever this was chasing after me, no matter how tired and crabby I may have felt.

"Jon," I said as he came running toward me, a paper in one hand and a pen in the other. Jon V., as we all called him, was the principal of our small Ocean County school, but he also did some work for our corporate office, helping place equipment orders for the other schools and running our central resource library.

"Ellyn," he said again, finally catching up to me. He seemed a little out of breath. "Sorry to stop you on your way out. But I need you to sign off on this and I wasn't sure when you'd be back in the office again."

I put my briefcase down on the floor, my folders on the receptionist's desk. "No problem, Jon," I said to him, taking the paper from his hand and scanning it. There wasn't much on it, just a list of book titles and computer models. "What am I looking at here?"

"That's the supplies from the Somerset storage facility that I'm going to send to our Maryland school," he told me, pointing to the items on the paper as I read it. Sending old equipment to our out-of-state schools was one of our regular practices, and Jon was largely in charge of it. "Discontinued and obsolete stuff we don't use anymore," he went on. "There's no room in our storage bins anymore thanks to all the new stuff we're getting, so I just need you to approve a FedEx shipment to get rid of it all."

He smiled wide, and I couldn't help but do the same. Something about organizing inventory just seemed to make this man happy, and I couldn't help finding that amusing.

"Sounds good," I told him, taking his pen and crossing out "FedEx" at the top of the sheet, "but please, use UPS—it's so much cheaper. Thank you for keeping on top of this, Jon. And for keeping the inventory of the library. How would we keep track of anything without you?"

As I handed back the edited shipping authorization form, he smiled still, and I swore he started to blush a little. "No problem, Ellyn. You have a good night, now," he replied, shaking the paper at me and then running off back down the hallway. When he was gone, I picked up my things and headed back toward the doorway, thoughts of the Somerset school, since he'd mentioned it, dancing in my head. That, I decided, was where I would head to tomorrow.

Five

If there's one thing I've learned during all my years as an educator, it's this: If you want to hear how great you are and have your ego stroked for a little while, ask your staff what they think of something you've done. If you want real, honest opinions, ask your students. They're never afraid to tell you what the real deal is.

With that in mind, during the first week of April 2004, I brought a group of kids from the old Somerset school to the new Somerset school to show them around and, more importantly, find out if they liked the place. I was pretty impressed with what we were building there, as were my colleagues, but I realized that none of that would make a lick of difference if this new facility wasn't appealing to the students.

Standing in the middle of what I'd dubbed the "Main Street" area of the school—a big, open space lined by various rooms, mostly empty but some already starting to fill up with furniture and equipment—I watched as the students started investigating. It was a small group, a few kids from each grade who I thought would get a lot out of this new school's programs.

"So, girls," I said, approaching a couple of juniors—Anna and Monique, both of whom I had an eye on for our dental assistant training lab for the following year. I'd known them since they'd started at New Road and had always liked them; they were opinionated and headstrong, smart girls who didn't take any flack from anyone. They were fighters, and I felt proud that my schools were giving them a fighting chance in life.

"What do you think?" I asked them, holding my breath and waiting for their responses. It was so important to me that they liked this place—and if they didn't, it was important that I find out why.

They'd been peering inside a large, darkened room housing a

couple of large machines, but they leaned back out at the sound of my voice.

"It looks cool, Dr. Lerner," said Anna, putting one hand on her hip and twirling a lock of her brown hair with the other, "but what is it? What are *those* for?"

"Those are embroidery machines," I told her, reaching inside the room to flip on the light switch. "This is going to be a workshop where students will take orders from businesses or individuals outside the school and make embroidered T-shirts and hats, that sort of thing."

"Ohhh," Monique said, looking at Anna. Their faces were lighting up, and it made my heart skip a beat. Two students won over—only a few hundred more to go. "That's cool. So we'll actually be making money if we work here?"

I laughed. Teenagers are always looking for an extra buck, and my students were no exception. "Not exactly," I explained. "The school will get the money and it will go toward maintaining the equipment and whatever else we need. But you will get a lot of good experience that you'll be able to go out and find a job with once you graduate."

"Can I work here?" Anna asked, gazing at the mysterious machines.

"We'll see," I replied, visions of the yet-to-be-finished dental lab floating through my head. I could just picture these two in white coats and rubber gloves, learning how to do impressions and read X-rays. I loved what we were building here in the Main Street area, but that lab, along with the optical lab and our other new programs, was really where my heart lay. "Let's see what the best fit is for you once September comes. You'll work with your teacher, your counselor and your parents to pick a major and a minor, and then we'll adjust your individualized education program and course of study to work around that."

After giving each of them a friendly squeeze on the shoulder, I left them to continue examining the embroidery machines and wandered over to another curious group—this one boys, both juniors. When they started at this school in the fall, they would be seniors, and I tried to picture which programs would be right for them. For Wadell, a seventeen-year-old who had been with New Road for a couple of years, I imagined a spot in the pharmacology lab. He was a good student and seemed to have a mind for math and science. James, who was sixteen, was a whiz on the Internet, and I never saw him without some sort of handheld game system in his grip. He would most likely benefit from our improved computer repair class or our Internet wiring class. He'd also do great in our technology-training lab, where he could earn A+ certification, a gateway for employment in the technology field.

Both boys were looking eagerly into what would eventually be our video store but was right now just a small room with a counter and a cash register.

"Dr. Lerner, what's this gonna be?" James asked as he saw me coming over, pulling out one of his earphones as he spoke to me. In his hand he clutched a small iPod and though, normally, I would have told him to put it away, this was a special occasion. If he needed a little musical accompaniment to see the greatness of this place, then so be it.

"It's going to be a store where you can buy DVDs," I told him with a smile. "And maybe video games, too. We're still looking into that."

"No kidding!" was his quick reply as he peered back into the room, visualizing, I imagined, the walls lined with movies and games. "But, uh…" He turned back to me then, his eyes squinting as his mind worked on forming the question. "How much are they going to cost?"

"Yeah," Wadell piped in. "I don't get much allowance. Mom says I don't help out around the house enough, so she doesn't want to give me any money."

I laughed at that and so did James, though he was nodding in agreement as though it happened to him all the time, too. They were typical teenagers, and I was sure that they were more concerned with hanging out with their friends than making sure that all the dishes were done at home.

James answered Wadell for me: "Man, you can use your behavior modification points and the New Road School money to buy this stuff. Right, Dr. Lerner?"

"Exactly," I told them, pleased that he had caught on so quickly. "You already have your behavior plan where you earn points and 'school money' for behavior and work completion." They both nodded. "Well, we'll have the same thing here, but like a hundred and ten percent cooler. Here, you'll still get to work your way up the levels when you do good work and get the same basic rewards and privileges. But you'll also get New Road money that you can spend here, inside the school—rather than having to order things from outside like you do now."

"So I could take my money and spend it here, at the movie store?" James asked, looking back into the empty room.

"Or at the pet store, or the photo shop, or the nail salon, though I don't think that one will be a big draw for you guys." They politely laughed at my joke, and then I added, "Or, you can put it in our bank and save it. You'll even earn interest, and can make withdrawals whenever you want to."

I looked around us, at all the nearly empty rooms, and envisioned what this would be some day soon—a true marketplace for our students where they could not only learn valuable career skills but take part in a working economy as well. Though the money they gained through the behavior program wouldn't be good anywhere else, it would still be a tangible reward, something to teach them how it felt to have a hard-earned dollar in their pocket—a feeling I hoped they would take with them once they were out of school and in the real, working world.

The Main Street micro-society was a pretty revolutionary concept; it was bigger and better than anything we'd tried in any of our facilities. Never before had we tried a behavior modification plan that was so all-encompassing and far-reaching, affecting all areas of the kids' educational experience. But this was par for the course at New Road, where we prided ourselves on innovation—and where I believe I did an enormous amount of innovative work. As I always had, even before New Road, I looked for the newest and best to offer our students and went as far as I could to give them everything they needed at a higher caliber than any other school could.

This attitude, over the years, had brought me a great amount of respect not only from my peers in the educational field but from the communities surrounding our schools. I'd had articles written about me in local newspapers; in 2002, I'd won the Association of Education Practitioners and Providers' James P. Boyle Entrepreneurial Leadership Award. I enjoyed good relationships with state agencies, partially because New Road consistently outperformed other organizations in our field; out of 175 special needs schools in New Jersey, New Road held some of the cheapest tuitions (ranking tenth, sixteenth and thirtieth) and had the most to offer when it came to basic instruction, higher-level academic electives coursework, and career-training services. And that was even before we opened our new flagship facilities with all the new training labs and this, our Main Street marketplace.

More importantly, though, my innovations sat right with my students. These kids appreciated what I did for them, and on top of that, they enjoyed it. They enjoyed having more choices and more challenges than their friends who went to other schools. They knew they had more opportunities at New Road than they would have anywhere else, and I know that they appreciated that. They appreciated their teachers and their newly found confidence and competence. They appreciated *me,* and I was just as happy to be the one who gave them so many opportunities.

Six

A week later, our Parlin office was raided and as I've already made pretty clear, I just did not see it coming. I was giving tours of the new schools and going about the normal, everyday business of keeping New Road up, running and thriving. My only concerns were getting the two new facilities done to spec and on time and ensuring that our three New Jersey schools continued to offer top-of-the-line educational opportunities to our students. New Road was my life, my love, and I never would have intentionally let anything bad happen to it.

Though as I was beginning to realize on that Monday afternoon, maybe that decision was not up to me. After investigator Ben Kukis had confined me to the conference room so I couldn't *collaborate* with any of my so-called *accomplices,* I had a lot of time to think about the situation, to try to figure out just what was happening despite the lack of information I had been given about it. There was a search warrant, and evidence was being collected, but that was basically all I knew. Once I'd demanded to see my lawyer, that Kukis fellow had become more tight-lipped than ever, and so I really knew next to nothing about what was going on there.

Still, I thought and thought and thought about it, and I wondered: *Should* I have seen it coming? Should I have known that we were doing something so serious, so vile, that it would require a whole law enforcement team to uncover it? Was there something we'd been doing that I should have picked up on? Should I have suspected one of my employees of some sort of...what, sabotage? Criminality? Fraud? I just couldn't imagine what any of us could have done to warrant this Gestapo invasion.

Even though I was being treated like a criminal already, in my heart of hearts I knew that I'd done nothing wrong. In all my many years in education, I'd never done anything below the board, nothing that would have in any way jeopardized the students, the teachers or the schools that I had vowed to help, had spent half my lifetime helping. Someone like me just didn't get into situations like this; I was a well-liked, well-respected, active and *effective* member of the New Jersey educational system, and my first concern had always been my students. Everyone in the field knew that!

So, what is it? I thought, my mind spinning like the conference-room chair on which I sat, turning and turning as I tried to figure out what was going on there. Kukis hadn't been back to check on me at all, not since I'd told him I wanted my lawyer. Hours passed, and I wondered if my staff was still being held prisoner in the gym upstairs.

Four hours into it, a lawyer did show up—a Mr. Townsend, sent over by Robert Kipnees from the firm that regularly represented New Road. In all honesty I barely knew Robert and I'd never met Townsend before, mostly because New Road had never really had any legal trouble before—just the usual, run-of-the-mill employee issues. Robert's firm had done our incorporation work, our partnership agreements, our by-laws and our employment law issues and we kept them on retainer basically as a formality, and so we always had someone to fall back on when we needed advice with contracts or regulations. None of them— or us—had ever had reason to believe that we would be involved in something like this.

"Ellyn," Mr. Townsend said, shaking my hand and putting his briefcase down on the table. "I just got done talking to Ben Kukis, the lead investigator."

"You did?" I said eagerly, gesturing to him to sit down, though I had to remain standing myself. Being so close to a possible explanation of these events had me so nervous, I just wanted to pace a bit. "What did he tell you? Did he tell you why they're tearing apart our offices?"

Townsend sighed and he did sit down, pulling, as he did so, another copy of the search warrant from the outer pocket of his briefcase. He held it up to me. "You get one of these?"

I nodded. "Yeah. I read it, but to be honest with you I don't really get it."

"Well, what it says," he began, and then I did slowly sink down into a chair, feeling my knees growing a little weak. After all the insane notions that had passed through my head since the moment I'd seen those gray Crown Victorias outside earlier that morning, I was prepared for the worst but dreaded hearing it anyway.

"Putting it simply," Townsend went on, "one of your employees went to the DOJ and reported that you're mishandling New Road's money."

I looked at him blankly for a moment, giving his words time to sink in to my brain. "Mishandling the *money?*" I finally asked him, the only thing I was able to say. What money was this Kukis talking about? Our petty cash fund? That sat in a lockbox in my office closet, but I rarely even touched it—I left that up to Kathy, my assistant, or Jill, the receptionist. And though there was no way that either of them would have done anything wrong with it, a mistake was always possible… But no, that was only a few hundred bucks, nothing that would have caused this much of an uproar

What was it, then? Was someone stealing? Embezzling? It certainly couldn't have had anything to do with our ordering of school supplies. Could it have been a non-allowable cost in our budget? No, that would have been checked and caught by our financial people and then rechecked by our outside auditors.

"You're gonna have to explain this to me, Mr. Townsend," I told the lawyer, closing my eyes to stop my head from spinning. "I really have no idea what you're talking about."

Taking a pair of reading glasses out of his inside jacket pocket, he put them on and then unfolded the search warrant along with several pages of notes that Ben Kukis had given him. Flipping through the pages, he looked for the official explanation for this chaos. Finally, he stopped, his eyes scanning a dog-eared page, his face calm and concentrated.

"Well, it says here in the investigator's notes," he said, pausing to clear his throat, "that a former employee of yours went to the state's deputy attorney general's office last month and told them that you and New Road are employing…" He glanced at the paper, pulling it away a little bit to bring the words into focus. "*Improper or illegal practices.*"

He dropped the papers on the table and slowly took off his reading glasses, then finally looked straight at me. "According to Kukis, this employee said that you're giving out illegal bonuses concealed as regular compensation, that you're shipping school supplies bought with New Jersey's money to out-of-state schools, and that you're cheating the state out of money by upping your spending at the end of the year in order to zero out your accounts and avoid sending anything back to the state."

If I hadn't already been sitting down, I surely would have had to at that point, because this—this just was not what I'd been expecting. Yes, I had covered all sorts of disastrous scenarios in my mind, but what Townsend was saying was just so far off the deep end, it was practically unbelievable. Illegal bonuses? Making New Jersey pay for supplies for my schools in other states? Zeroing out as cheating? These were ludicrous accusations. This was a scandal. An outrage.

I took a deep breath, slowly in and out through my nose, trying to focus my anger and get a grip on it. "Is that it?" I asked him.

He nodded, eyeing me as though wary that I might jump up and start screaming. "That's all he told me. Frankly, I think that it's enough."

I laughed at that but bitterly, because there really was not one funny thing about this. New Road had been the target of a few frivolous lawsuits over the years, generally from disgruntled ex-employees who wanted a little something for nothing. This could have been just that, but it didn't feel like it to me. This wasn't simply someone trying to get us to settle and throw some cash at them. This was a *raid*. An *investigation*. And it was authorized by the deputy attorney general.

This was done by someone who really had it in for New Road—or maybe just for me.

"Who's saying all this?" I asked. "Who's the employee making the accusations?"

He picked up the notes from Kukis again and flipped some more pages, then put his reading glasses back on. "That would be…" he began as he looked for the name, his excruciating slowness almost killing me. "Oh. Here it is. The whistleblower is someone named…Pamela Hall."

"Pamela Hall?" I shouted. "*Pamela Hall?* How did she—what did she—" In my shock, I couldn't even form a sentence. Never in a million years would I have guessed that she would have caused this big of a fuss. Yes, her job performance hadn't been the highest; she'd had some personality conflicts around the office. But could she bring something like this down upon New Road? It boggled my mind—and infuriated me.

"Who was she?" Townsend asked, again abandoning the search warrant on the table and removing his glasses.

I sighed and rubbed my temples, a searing headache beginning to blossom behind my forehead. "She was our controller. She worked here for about a year and a half, not long, and she just quit in March. It seemed to me like she had a lot of problems, and the level of responsibility Mark put on her might have been too much."

Suddenly, I remembered the way Mark used to berate Pamela, the arguments they used to have. When she'd left, it had been sudden, and though she'd only cited personal and health issues as the reasons for her departure, I'd wondered if Mark's badgering had had something to do with it. Most normal people had trouble bearing the brunt of his so-called humor on a good day. Pamela seemed fragile, high strung, maybe a little paranoid. It seemed to me that she had struggled with her job duties, and that gave Mark a lot of fodder to use against her. The two had been a bad match; that much had been clear. We probably shouldn't have kept her on as long as we had.

"Was she a troublemaker of some sort?" Townsend asked me.

"I wouldn't say that," I replied. "But trouble did sort of seem to find her. She dug herself into a lot of holes around here, and she'd mentioned from time to time that she'd had some problems in her personal life. She came into the office visibly upset some days. Sometimes, I asked her a question and she just stared off into space for a minute before answering me, like her mind was just somewhere else entirely."

Maybe that was when I should have let her go, I thought ruefully.

But I hadn't, because that just wasn't me. I'd always practiced "kind confrontation" with employees when their work appeared to be suffering, along with improvement plans and probation periods that included frequent assistance and supervision. It was only when I could no longer build their confidence and competence, contribute to their greatness and demonstrate a genuine affinity towards them that it was time to terminate.

Unfortunately, I'd never been able to do any of those things with Pamela Hall, and certainly Mark hadn't either—it just wasn't in his nature. What's more, if I ever even tried to help Pamela, he blew up at me, accusing me of trying to do end-runs around him. I should have forced him to cut the strings on Pamela as soon as I'd realized that but

I didn't, and the tension in their department just grew and grew; it was palpable and I believe it affected Pamela's work negatively. To me, she'd seemed totally overwhelmed by the requirements of the job and her personal issues. She appeared to be drowning. Still, she'd never come to me with any issues. So, what could I have done?

Mr. Townsend nodded sympathetically, as if he'd dealt with that particular breed of difficult employee himself. "Honestly, I wasn't sorry to see her go when she quit. In fact, I was happy. But this? This *whistle-blowing*? These charges just don't make sense. It's ridiculous, all of it, and I never would have suspected she'd be capable of it."

Mr. Townsend shrugged at me. "People can be surprising," he said blandly.

Before I could voice any further outrage, the door of the conference room opened and a young man—assumedly one of the investigation team—told Mr. Townsend that Detective Kukis wanted to speak with him.

"Alright," Townsend said, standing up and straightening his suit. "Ellyn, now that I'm here you can make phone calls, so if you need to reach anyone, perhaps now would be the time."

"Sure, thanks," I said, already reaching for the phone as he walked out of the room. I called Mark on his cell phone. When he'd gotten word about what was going on here, he'd turned right around and gone back home.

"Pamela Hall?" he asked when I filled him in on the claims she'd made against us, then let out a string of expletives, most of them describing Pamela.

"I know, it's unbelievable," I agreed, shaking my head. I still couldn't wrap my mind around the entire thing, even as it was happening around me.

He gave a nervous laugh. "Yeah, well... I know you're going to kill me for not telling you this..."

"Not telling me what, Mark?" I asked, an edge creeping into my voice. I really didn't need any further surprises at the moment.

"Listen, I never thought it was relevant, and it probably isn't. But, do you remember Pamela Hall's previous employer?" I thought for a moment. "Village Networks, Inc.?" I remembered seeing it on her résumé. The name had stood out to me because the company's headquarters was very close to my house.

"That's the one. She was the controller there, too. Do you know what happened to Village Networks?"

"No, I know nothing about it. Was it part of the tech bubble?"

"No," Mark mumbled through the phone. He'd always been a bit of a mumbler, especially when put on the spot. "It went under. *Someone* accused the company of stealing trade secrets from Lucent. They were raided by the FBI—their offices and their homes."

I remained silent, an idea forming in my head. "Are you saying Pamela was the whistleblower there, too?" It seemed unbelievable—but too much of a coincidence to overlook.

"I'm not saying that for sure, because who knows? I never thought anything of it when I interviewed her. She never said anything that made me think she was responsible. And I looked the company up on the Internet at the time, and I don't remember her being mentioned. But it's suspiciously similar to the situation we're in right now, don't you think?"

I sat back in my chair and crossed my arms over my chest. "Yes, I do," I agreed as the conference door opened and Mr. Townsend came back in. He sat down across from me, next to the phone, which I had on speaker. "She'll find nothing wrong here," I added.

Mark and I chatted about Pamela for another couple of minutes, remembering some of the more bizarre moments of her career at New Road. I usually made it my policy to talk only about the good in people, but Pamela had been a strange young woman, and I was sort of kicking myself now for not seeing the signs earlier.

When our call was over, I turned my attention back to Mr. Townsend. "So? What did he want?"

"Just a couple of points from our earlier conversation he wanted clarified," he explained. "Nothing to worry about." He eyed me sternly. "How are you holding up?"

I sighed and rested my head on my hand. "I'm tired," I said. "I want to get out of here."

He nodded and smiled, looking sincerely sympathetic. "You will," he said. "We have to be patient. Investigations of this sort often take time. They take on a life of their own."

I had no idea what that meant, but I laughed a little anyway because for the time being, at least I knew what was going on and could stop imagining the worst. I even began to feel like this was all just a big misunderstanding and that it would blow over before long, once they realized that Pamela's charges were absurd. New Road was regularly audited by a very thorough outside firm that we'd been using for years, and we had had a history of superb state monitoring reviews that showed our accounting department's and our auditors' compliance with all rules and regulations. We had so many layers of checks, I just couldn't imagine anything having gone that terribly awry.

"They won't find any wrongdoing at all," I told Mr. Townsend assuredly, shaking my head. "I'm not hiding anything. And it won't take them long to see that they've got nothing on me."

When I left the building that night a little after ten o'clock, the parking lot was empty. Kukis was just pulling out in his Crown Victoria as I reached my own car, and in the distance I saw red taillights receding, probably the last of my employees racing toward home. I shook my head, so annoyed that they'd been treated so badly, that they'd gotten caught up in this whirlwind of misunderstanding.

Kukis had kept me sequestered all day and left everyone else in the gym, allowing us out one by one for supervised bathroom breaks, just like we were in prison. Robert Kipnees had called several times to check up on us and his associate, Mr. Townsend, stayed for quite a while, going in and out of the conference room and acting as my intermediary with the investigation team. No new revelations came up for the rest of the day; the workers were pretty tight-lipped about their mission and simply packed up anything they could get their hands on, including all of our computers and fifty-eight boxes full of files.

Whatever good that will do them, I thought as I got into my car. They could take everything out of our offices—papers, hard drives, filing cabinets, furniture, whatever—and they still wouldn't be able to make a case against New Road because we simply had not done anything wrong.

On the drive home, I tried not to think about it all too much and instead kept my mind on the road. I was exhausted both mentally and physically, and by the time I pulled into my garage all I could think about was taking a hot shower and crawling into bed. Maybe I'd have some good dreams to wash this whole nightmare away.

Inside, I found my husband, Alan, in the living room. The TV was off and there was no noise whatsoever, like he was just sitting there in vigil, waiting for my return. My daughters, Erica and Melissa, had come in from New York once they'd heard that New Road had been raided, and they ran downstairs now, the looks of worry on their faces almost bringing me to tears. The way they rushed over to hug me didn't help either.

"I'm fine, I'm fine," I told them, wondering why they had come in the first place and why everyone looked so somber. Through Robert Kipnees, I'd gotten word to Alan during the day about what was going on at the Parlin school; I'm sure Rob hadn't gone into too much detail, but he did say that I was being detained and would probably be home late. Okay, given that, I could understand their worry. But by that time, I'd convinced myself so well that the situation was not as bad as it seemed, I just didn't see the need to make such a fuss.

"Well, come on, tell us what's going on," Melissa said, leading me into the living room, her sister trailing behind us. I sat down on the sofa next to Alan, and he took my hand and smiled at me reassuringly, though I could tell that he was eager to hear what the problem was.

So, I told them all the entire story from beginning to end—the cars in the parking lot in the morning, the cop escorting me to the gym, the solitary confinement of the conference room, Kukis and the other twenty or so investigators, Mr. Townsend and, finally, Pamela Hall's allegations. Alan especially had heard my complaints about her before—who can we gripe about work to if not our spouses?—but even he was shocked to hear that she was responsible for this.

"I thought she was just kind of a harmless sad sack," he offered, and his description made me laugh.

I shrugged. "So did I," I said. "Apparently she had something brewing under the surface that none of us knew about. But at least no charges were filed, and no one is under arrest. It's just an investigation into the accusations and honestly I don't think that anything will come of it."

"Mom, I don't either," Erica quickly interjected. "I wouldn't worry about *any* of it if I were you. You never do anything wrong. You're like...*perfect*. No, seriously, all the work you do is so awesome, how can anybody say that you're doing something bad?"

I smiled at her and ran a hand over her hair. She was so smart, so beautiful, so supportive of everything I did, just like her sister and her dad. I looked around at them all and wondered how I ever would have made it so far in life without them. For as much as I adored New Road and everything I had accomplished with it, of course I loved my family a hundred times more. My girls, my husband—my *family*—meant the world to me, more than any award or achievement or recognition for the work I'd done ever could. My family was my real pride and joy, the thing that I could rely on above all else, even when everything was hitting the fan, and that gave me comfort that night. Because I didn't know yet just how much more was going to be thrown at me.

Seven

The next morning, the New Road offices looked like a war zone—papers everywhere, furniture moved all around, nothing where it should have been. My staff walked around shell-shocked, their eyes wide, their voices silent. No one knew what to say about what had happened there.

And neither did I. Standing in front of my bare desk—Kukis and his team had taken everything, from my computer to my coffee-stained calendar blotter—I couldn't do anything but shake my head and wonder, yet again, what was going on. The drawers of my filing cabinets were opened and empty; even the plants on the windowsills had been moved. These people had left nothing untouched, as if even my pen cup might have held some sort of evidence.

I walked slowly around the desk and sat down on my chair, one of the few familiar objects that remained. Taking it all in, all the carnage that lay before me, all the time it would take to get ourselves back on track, I lay my palms flat on the desktop to try to steady myself. My head spun slightly, and I began to feel a slight twinge of doubt.

Maybe this is serious, I thought. *Maybe this is worse than I thought.*

"Knock, knock," Dave said from the doorway, and I waved him in. He walked over toward my desk, surveying my decimated office as he made his way through it.

"How's yours looking?" I asked him.

He shrugged. There was no humor in him, nor was there any hint of his usual sarcasm. "About the same," he replied, finally looking over at me. "Just came in to see how you're doing."

I shrugged, too. What else could I do? "I'm okay," I told him, though in reality I was working pretty hard to keep myself from giving in to panic. "I'm okay," I repeated, as if saying it again would make it true.

He nodded, his eyes wandering around the room again, stopping for a moment on the overturned wastebasket. "So what exactly happened here yesterday, Ellyn?"

The tone of his voice—not exactly accusatory, but not entirely sympathetic, either—was not lost on me. He knew what had happened. He'd come in late, but he'd been there, separated off into his own room, unable to talk to anyone, just like I had been. I was sure that Mr. Townsend had run down the charges with him just like he had with me. There was no way that Dave did not know what was going on.

I sighed. "Well, they think we've been...*mishandling* New Road's money."

Dave shut his eyes tightly and brought his fingertips up to rub them. "Yeah, I got that yesterday. But what does that mean?" He opened his eyes again and blinked at me, bringing me back into focus. "I mean, we're not, are we? We're not mishandling anything."

I shrugged and smiled. "Not that I know of."

"Well, what about the bonuses? She said we're giving out bonuses."

She, I thought. I wondered if we would ever say Pamela Hall's name out loud again or if she would now be relegated to a mere pronoun, an unspeakable enemy.

"We're not," I told him calmly. "It's our contingent pay structure policy. Either she didn't know our company practices or misunderstood them, or she merely took this one out of context."

For many years, New Road had built into its employee compensation plan a sort of incentive program. If the school did better than expected in terms of enrollment increases, then every employee got a "contingent pay" increase. It was part of each staff member's employment contract, and it had been approved by our lawyers, our auditors and everyone else who had looked at it—including Pamela Hall, who had been hired to maintain such internal controls. Now, she was saying that it was somehow wrong, that it went against the state regulations. The same ones she had been repeatedly reprimanded for not knowing.

"And the end-of-year spending?"

"Same thing," I told him. "You know that we try to use up whatever money we have left at the end of the year so we don't have to send money back to the state. Dave, I don't know a state-funded agency that *doesn't* do that. It's ludicrous that we'd be investigated for it. We're spending the money on school supplies and programs—nothing that isn't allowed."

Waiting until the last quarter of the fiscal year to do most of the large purchasing was not an unheard-of practice; many state-funded agencies did just that because as far as budgeting went, it was the easiest way to handle it. In the fourth quarter, you know what you will have left over once all the necessities are taken care of, so you know what you can and cannot afford. If we did all our purchasing and found that there was still money in our budget, we returned it. It just happened that we rarely had anything left over—but we did have schools that were known for their state-of-the-art facilities. To me, that was what really mattered.

Dave nodded thoughtfully, looking around again at the office. The night before, Townsend had handed me an itemized list of everything the investigators had taken, pages and pages and pages of stuff. At the time I'd thought the list was a little exaggerated, but seeing this all in the light of day, I now wondered if there was anything he'd left off of it.

"They said we're sending books to our schools in other states," he went on.

"And we are," I conceded, starting to feel a little more confidence, a little less despair. Talking about all this reminded me that we *hadn't* done anything wrong, that we were completely above the board, that Kukis and his cronies would have nothing on us in the end. "But they're outdated and we don't use them anymore. They're books from the school pods and computers that we don't use anymore—the stuff that's in storage. It's all obsolete or discontinued here and we just give them to our smaller out-of-state schools to use as extra independent work or to preview for wide-scale purchase. I can't imagine that goes against any rule or regulation."

We looked at each other for a moment, both of us unsure what should come next.

"Kipnees is expecting us at his office at eleven to go over all this," Dave finally said, breaking the silence. He looked blankly around the office one last time, then back at me. "I imagine you'll be available?"

I laughed. For once, I was thankful to hear his biting commentary.

———

At the meeting, our lawyers gave us one salient piece of advice: Do not talk to anyone. If Kukis or anyone else from the Department of Justice contacted us, we were to tell them to call Robert Kipnees. Any correspondence, any inquiries or requests were to be directed to either him or his associates. It felt sort of good to have that buffer around us, to know that Kukis could not touch us. Though I was pretty convinced that this so-called investigation would come down to nothing, it was reassuring to have a good team of attorneys on our side.

Still, as the days wore on and we heard nothing from Kukis, I began to grow just the slightest bit paranoid. I began looking at everything we did, everything we had ever done, with a critical eye. Would our shipment of water for the office cooler be seen as an unnecessary expense? Could our policy of reimbursing employees for mileage when they traveled for their jobs come under scrutiny? Given the claims that Pamela Hall had made against us—and the DOJ's willingness to believe them—it seemed to me like nothing was safe anymore. Never again would I sign off on a purchase or institute a policy without thinking twice about it.

The whole thing also made me seriously reconsider just how much I took advantage of the gray areas in our state regulations. For example, because of the codes under which we operated, New Road could not pay for meals served at trainings or for any meetings held outside the state—at least not with money that New Jersey gave us. However, because New Road was a multi-state corporation we had various areas from which to pull funds, and not all the other states we worked with were as strict. So, we often had our meetings catered and even held a leadership training in Bermuda once, but none of it was on New Jersey's dime. It was all billed to our out-of-state entities. Was this legal? Yes. Was it ethical? I thought so, though other people might have disagreed. I was pretty sure that Ben Kukis would be among them.

Thoughts like these ate away at my conscience, robbing me of sleep and disturbing whatever peace of mind I might have had left. What if something in our accounting had been filed incorrectly? Could I even have proven that I hadn't ordered someone to do the New Jersey bookkeeping in the wrong manner? What if one of our less-diligent bookkeepers—or even Pamela Hall herself—had misunderstood my directions to charge the food, entertainment or leadership conference trips to an out-of-state entity? What if one of them even willfully entered the wrong information in the New Jersey books? How would I even know until it was too late?

Day after day I brought these paranoid questions to the accountants and asked them to look things up for me, to reassure me that everything had been billed properly, that there wasn't a stray invoice for a hotel room in Bermuda in among the New Jersey papers. But these girls were good. They had everything in order and were well aware of our governing state regulations. They reassured me that I had nothing to worry about and, really, all I could do at that point was believe them.

Eight

A year later, the investigation was still ongoing. Let me say that again: *A year later, the investigation was still ongoing.*

Though I'd somehow convinced myself in April 2004 that the whole thing would blow over within a matter of days, when weeks turned into months and there was still no resolution, I got the hint. This was more than a mere misunderstanding; it wasn't just going to go away. It was a battle and we were in it for the long haul, with no end in sight.

After the initial raid, I tried my best to get things back in order in the office. I put all the remaining papers back inside my filing cabinets and bought myself a new calendar; I straightened out my plants and everything else the investigators had knocked out of place. We were told that we would get our computers back within three days, but it was two weeks before the investigators called our IT in to pick them up. Finally, we were all able to get on with our work.

And from that point on, I went right along as if nothing had happened because what else could I do? I spent as much time at the schools as was humanly possible; I found great solace in the voices of our students, in the faces of our educators. When I immersed myself in the academic side of things and steered clear of the business office, I could almost pretend that New Road wasn't in any danger at all.

But in the back of my mind, it worried me constantly. I smiled and laughed and chitchatted. I met with contractors to keep on building out our new facilities, to make them bigger and better. I signed off on purchases and did my due diligence with our regular auditors when I had to. I held academic workshops and leadership retreats. I did everything I was supposed to, but I never let anyone see how much fear the investigation instilled in me. Sure, everything was okay for the time being, but I knew that it could all change in an instant. All Kukis needed was one shred of evidence to play with, one damning drop to drown us with.

Looking back, I suppose it was only a matter of time before that façade I worked so hard to maintain started to show some cracks.

———

Long spans of time passed without a word from anyone—not from Kukis, not our lawyers, the auditors or anyone else who had a finger in this great big messy pie—and I sometimes had no idea what was happening from one day to the next. Every morning I had to restrain myself from calling Robert Kipnees to beg him for information; I tried to limit myself to reaching out to him once or twice a week. My need for reassurance or "talk therapy" was becoming too expensive.

"Rob," I said warmly into the phone one September afternoon, shortly after school had started up for the year. I was in my office but not for long, just putting in a few hours before I headed out to our brand-new Somerset facility, which had just opened for business. The new Parlin school was up and running, too, and I couldn't have been prouder of both of them. These were great accomplishments for me both personally and professionally, and a giant collective leap for New Road as well. Unfortunately, the unbridled happiness I should have felt over them was tainted by the ongoing investigation—as everything in my life was at that moment.

"Tell me something good," I said, trying to keep the pleading tone out of my voice.

On the other end, he sighed a little. I didn't think he'd meant for me to hear it, but I did, and it deflated me. It was the sound of hope being lost, of optimism going right out the window. I imagined that he was just as tired of this whole case as I was, but still. I needed reassurance, and he was the only one who could give it.

"Have you heard from Kukis?" I pressed him. "Or from Mr. Rosner?"

Rosner was the prosecutor in charge of our case at the time and he'd already initiated a few exchanges with our attorneys, but even from him, information was not exactly forthcoming.

"Not a word," he replied. "Not in a while. Time is always on the side of the defense—I've told you that. Until the prosecution gets some momentum, or some indication that there's something to prosecute, we're in much better shape if we stay low. We don't want paint targets on our backs. In the meantime, though, have you and David considered our recommendation to call in a forensic accountant?"

Rob had told me a few weeks earlier that we should think about having an outside CPA look at our case and give a professional opinion on it—on the accusations, on New Road's innocence and on Pamela Hall's accountability in the matter.

"We talked about it. Do you really think it's a good idea?"

I could practically hear his shrug through the phone. "Can't hurt at this point, can it? I mean, you swear up and down that you haven't done anything wrong, and we back you up on that. Our firm's had a long enough relationship with New Road, and we know how you guys operate. This would just be a good objective source of validation for you—especially since we have no indication of what evidence the state has. Or thinks it has."

I nodded again. It made sense. "We'll get it done as soon as possible," I told him, and then I let him go, off the hook until the next time my insecurities got the best of me.

———

Nick Magone, the CPA we hired to look at our internal controls and accounting practices in light of Ben Kukis' investigation, spent a month in our main office in Parlin, talking to our employees and looking at all of our books. At the end of it, he wrote up a briefing paper that he submitted to Rob Kipnees and associates, the gist of which was this: New Road had done nothing wrong. If the finger of blame pointed at anyone, it was Pamela Hall.

In detail, Magone reviewed how Pamela had come to work at New Road. In 2002, because Mark's role as CFO was focusing more on business development and client management, we decided to hire a controller to oversee our internal controls, such as our policies and procedures and our adherence to state standards. As our new controller and a certified public accountant, Pamela Hall also would be the primary accounting officer responsible for New Road's daily transactions, including properly documenting accounts payable into the correct schools and categories. For example, we didn't want the consumable school supplies billed with the non-instructional equipment. Also, we wanted to ensure that supplies ordered for Delaware were billed to the Delaware school and not to Maryland, New Jersey or DC. Those were the primary accountabilities for which Pamela Hall was to develop the internal controls, as indicated in her contract and job description in June 2002.

Having worked as an outside auditor for some fairly high-profile corporations before coming to New Road, Pamela appeared more than capable of performing these duties, and Mark hired her with a good deal of expectations. In the previous few years New Road had grown by leaps and bounds, expanding both our physical facilities as well as our human resources, and in that time, our internal controls had kind of fallen by the wayside. Not that we weren't following them; we always obeyed all policies we were supposed to. We just hadn't expanded our controls sufficiently to keep up with the company's growth, and so we'd hired Pamela to work on that: to improve our systems, upgrade the way we operated and bring New Road into the next level of its well-oiled existence.

And maybe Pamela had intended to do all that. Maybe she came into the job with enthusiasm and an eagerness to get things done. But if she did, it didn't last for long, according to Magone's report.

During interviews with some of New Road's accounting staff who had worked with Pamela Hall, Nick Magone found out that Pamela often "rebuffed" anyone who had questions about our systems or controls and gave little guidance to those she should have been leading. One woman even claimed that Pamela ridiculed her. Unfortunately, none of these complaints ever reached my ears; if they had, I sure would have done something about them.

Hearing them now, did it surprise me? Not really. I'd known there'd been issues with getting Pamela up to speed on the state regulations, but I'd had no idea how deep the problem had gone. An example: Our accounts payable bookkeepers told Nick Magone that Pamela had originally told them to charge purchases to the people ordering them, not to the schools for which they were ordered—which was incorrect. Thankfully, the bookkeepers went to Mark and got the correct information. When they related this story to Nick, he got the distinct impression that our controller had been in way over her head.

This lack of proper information and sufficient internal controls, according to Magone's findings, was what led to any accounting problems that Kukis might have thought he'd found. If anything was not properly accounted for, Magone noted, "it was most likely because of new personnel and a lack of procedures or controls over the purchasing and quite possibly a lack of understanding of the regulations."

But was that New Road's fault? Or was it Mark's fault? Or Dave's? Could it have been mine? That was a question I grappled with throughout this ordeal. Were we—was I—responsible for the possible misconduct of our employees? Logically, I would say yes. In the environment I'd worked so hard to create, wherein we all supported and encouraged one another, I could say that the failure of one was the failure of all of us. But in this case, I just had a hard time believing it, not because I didn't want to take any blame on myself but because Pamela so obviously knew that she needed information and help. Yet, she never once came to me and asked for either. She merely dug herself deeper and deeper into a hole—then climbed out and trapped us in there instead.

Or at least, I imagined, that was what she was hoping to do. Nick Magone's report, I was sure, would negate all her accusations. Aside from the in-depth analysis of Pamela's performance and lack thereof, in his report he went into some detail about auditing procedures and how incredibly consistently New Road complied with the process. We didn't just meet the auditing standards; we provided our auditors with an exhaustive amount of documentation and free access to our files, our employees and our facilities. We did this because we relied upon these people to show us our weaknesses and noncompliances, to help us improve New Road and keep it running smoothly.

"Clearly," Magone wrote, "an organization or individual seeking to defraud would not provide such information to their auditors." He also noted that the auditors never reported any deficiencies with regard to our control structure or our management in general.

≈

Magone's report was a revelation of sorts, a solid piece of positive evidence for our arsenal. Reading it one afternoon at Robert Kipnees' office, I felt a bit bolstered, a little more capable of facing the continuing storm. At least we had something to show for ourselves, an expert opinion that said that we had done nothing wrong.

"Now if only we could give this to the banks," I said, tossing the report back onto Rob's desk, "maybe they'd leave us alone."

As soon as word of the investigation got out, New Road had been besieged on all sides and probably the worst of it had come from the banks: They'd called in the mortgages on our schools, an enormous sum that we would have been hard-pressed to pay outright.

"Have you worked anything out with them?" he asked me, his brow lowered in a most non-reassuring manner.

"We've held them off for now," I replied dejectedly, absently reaching out to thumb through the papers once more. "But they'll be back. They want us to pay up before we get too involved in a criminal case or a civil lawsuit or something and can't afford our payments anymore."

For months the threat of bankruptcy had loomed over my head like a thunderous black cloud, reminding me that everything I had worked so hard to build could be lost in an instant, even if no formal charges were ever filed against us. Just being involved in an investigation was costly; we'd already paid an arm and a leg for Magone's assessment and for five separate lawyers, one each for Dave, Mark, myself and each of the schools involved. We also had to enlist another attorney every time an employee was called to testify before the grand jury that Rosner had convened.

On top of that, Rob had suggested that we hire an educational specialist, say the head of a special education department at a local university, to evaluate the efficacy of our program. This would undoubtedly cost a great deal of money but an independent evaluation of our schools would serve to prove that as educators, we were among the top in the state.

I had no idea what sort of bill we would rack up if we ever actually had to go to trial, but I was sure it would exceed our already shaky credit limit.

"And the staff?" Rob asked. "How are they handling it?"

"Honestly, very few people outside the office even know what's happening. I guess that's a blessing in disguise."

"It can be," Rob agreed. "It probably makes it easier on you, anyway. You don't have people asking you all the time about what's going on."

And thankfully, that was true. Most of our employees—all except the administrative staff, the department heads and those authorized to get on the accounting software, which, ironically, I was not—were blissfully ignorant of the investigation or at least too shy to ask about it. If they did, I would tell them what was going on. I trusted everyone who worked for us and felt that if they wanted to know about it, then they had a right to.

Instead, it was the public at large that really worried me. Everyone knows how the media (not to mention the gossip grapevine) works, and I feared someone starting a campaign of misinformation against New Road. I was terrified that the school's reputation would be ruined if word ever got out that it was under investigation or, worse, if any charges were ever formalized. That was my first and foremost concern, even above the money or my own personal well-being. I just couldn't stand for New Road to be tainted in any way.

Leaving the attorneys' office with my head full of these thoughts, I decided to close out my day at Somerset. We were working on opening a new store in the Main Street area, and I wanted to check on its progress. Hoping that the distraction would lighten my mood a little, as I drove, I tried not to think about the investigation, the aftermath and, above all, Pamela Hall. But I couldn't help it. I just wanted to understand why she, as a human being, would do this to us. To New Road. To me.

Because, after all, this was my baby she was messing with.

Nine

To fully understand the possible charges and the criminal case that the prosecution wanted to bring forward, it is necessary to understand a highly simplified explanation of the extraordinarily unique approach to tuition-rate setting adopted by the New Jersey Department of Education over a decade ago. Prior to that time a flat-rate tuition (price-cap system) was employed wherein approved private schools serving students with special needs, such as New Road, received predetermined tuitions based on specific disability classifications.

When the Department of Education instituted the new set of regulations, however, they began stipulating what constituted allowable and non-allowable costs. The legislative intent of moving towards this new rate-of-return regulation (based on true costs plus a fixed rate of return) was aimed at (1) guaranteeing the fiscal solvency of the private schools, (2) ensuring that private schools made appropriate investments in each child's educational program, and (3) keeping tuition rates fair and reasonable through a process of disallowing certain costs that would unfavorably impact rate increases.

At the same time, districts were required to fund allowable excess expenditures (through a process known as *backbilling,* which is billing the district an amount equal to the overage) with virtually no limits on spending. This type of complex regulatory structure is frequently used for monopolies like the former telephone and electric companies to ensure that they invest in new technologies in order to offer customers better products, since there is no competition from which a customer may defect.

Rate-of-Return Regulation

The nuts and bolts of traditional rate-of return regulation are relatively simple. In form it is similar to a "cost plus" arrangement (e.g., allowable costs plus 2.5 percent of allowable costs). At its best, the rate-of-return regulation limits profits by guaranteeing a maximum return on investment. It also eliminates many of the risks associated with poorly performing investments (i.e., through backbilling if a private school spends more than its per-pupil allotment by the end of the year). However, this type of regulation provides an organization with little incentive not to be wasteful. Even if an organization spends more than necessary to produce a service, it still gets the same or an even greater profit through this backbilling process.

In other words, the primary problem of a regulatory system that is based on costs is the creation of perverse incentives—an organization can increase its costs and pass them on to its customers without diminishing its profit. To add insult to injury, a firm can earn even larger returns by simply *spending more money.*

As stated, the primary benefit of the rate-of-return regulatory system is found in near monopolies. It ensures investment so that operators cannot provide substandard products. However, where competition exists, the rate-of-return regulation creates a perverse effect of aggressively increasing operating costs so as to effectively provide the most (competitive) services for the most (aggressively expensive) cost.

Perverse Incentives

Under the New Jersey Department of Education's rate-of-return regulation, the consumers of the services—the school districts sending students to private schools for the disabled—bear all of the risks of cost increases, including any and all inefficiencies relating to poor investment decisions, poor purchasing processes and poor fiscal management.

Consider the following example:

> ABC Private School for the Disabled believes that
> an extensive dance-therapy program would increase

expression for students with communication-based learning disorders. To implement the program, ABC hires two dance therapists and two assistants and converts two classrooms into a dance therapy studio complete with mirrors, a state-of-the art sound system, wood flooring and soundproofing.

After two years of the program, one of the therapists leaves due to burnout. The school will have to offer a considerably higher salary to get a replacement with the same qualifications. In addition, the remaining dance therapist wants an increase to reflect the market-based salary offered to the replacement therapist.

ABC decides that the program is not worth the effort expended in finding qualified dance therapists as compared to the rewards of increased expressive communication or mobility gains for its students. ABC decides to discontinue the dance-therapy program and over the next year converts the dance studio into two classrooms. The current dance-therapy staff members are redeployed into an adaptive PE program.

The skyrocketing costs of this investment decision over the program's three to four years of implementation were passed on to the consumers—the public taxpayers and the school districts sending students to private special education placements. With no incentive to make prudent investment decisions and with a rate-of-return regulation in place, ABC Private School had no reason to evaluate the costs going into the program or choose less-expensive equipment such as the flooring or sound and soundproofing systems.

To add insult to injury, ABC actually increased its own benefit. Its surplus (either the fifteen-percent working-capital fund or the 2.5-percent surcharge) increased as a result of, for example, the costs associated with getting the most-expensive flooring, sound system and soundproofing and the higher salaries of the staff needed to perpetuate the experimental

program. Ironically, in New Jersey, a school organization can earn even larger returns by *simply spending
or even wasting more money,* thus the main implementation problem with rate-of-return regulation.

Despite the lack of incentive to minimize costs under New Jersey's
present system, the New Road organization had a goal to produce the
most cutting-edge programs at the least cost. We loved to brag about
being one of the lowest-cost providers in the entire state—we could
serve three kids in our facilities for the price of one student in other
schools—while still affording each child the very best in materials,
equipment, technology and innovative programs.

However, being a low-cost provider proved to have no worth whatsoever to the prosecutors who were hell-bent on showing wrongdoing
rather than praising thrift. Neither did our foregoing over $2.6 million
in backbilling over the ten-year period just prior to the onset of the
2004 investigation.

A school operator who understands this unique regulatory structure—especially one who strives to be the most competitive, least
expensive and most disciplined, and to absorb the loss of poor budgeting decisions rather than backbill— is not likely to engage in an illegal
practice in order to generate additional funds for his or her school. In
other words, why would we forego the legal and acceptable practice
of backbilling only to engage in an *illegal* practice that would generate zero additional funds over time and skew the tuition payments
towards an inflated amount in year one but a deflated amount in years
two through five? This would certainly constitute reasonable doubt in
any jury's mind if we chose to go to trial.

Furthermore, the Division of Criminal Justice never said that the
expenditures made on the equipment purchases (equipment for kitch-
ens for the two new school facilities, a gym and fitness center, an eye
lab, a dental lab, an engraving, embroidery and silk-screening production center and a driver's education facility) were in the non-allowable
category. They simply wanted them recorded as assets instead of supplies (expenses) and depreciated over five years rather than charged
into the tuition in year one only.

Our lawyers tried to stress to the prosecutors that the behavior
under scrutiny was very common amongst private schools. In all other

comparable cases, similar actions were not deemed criminal. They were either settled in civil court by reclassification and fines or administratively through the Department of Education, including fines, frozen tuition rates or conditional approval until a remedial plan would be approved. In no case was a school operator breaking down invoices to stay under a $2,000 threshold deemed criminal.

In the past thirty to forty years, since private schools were allowed in the State of New Jersey, there have only been two cases requiring criminal prosecution of private-school operators. Both were egregious actions involving a great deal of personal gain. In the first case, the owner was using state tuition money for his personal expenses, including landscaping at his home and purchasing a condo. In the second, the school owners used tuition dollars to pay for ten no-show jobs for friends and family to the tune of $150,000 per year apiece. Both of these cases were scrutinized by administrative review first before being handed up to the criminal courts.

However, New Road's case never went to administrative review. The criminal division took the case simply because Pamela Hall had gone directly to them. They never moved the case towards an administrative remedy nor did they ever consider civil charges, despite the fact that they acknowledged no personal gain and despite the reasonable doubt that surrounded their theories.

Ten

The deputy attorney general assigned to the New Road case was a man named Andrew Rosner and though I can't say that I liked him, I did respect him. At least, I do in retrospect. Compared to those who picked up the case later on, Rosner was a smart leader, capable of pursuing justice without turning it into a witch hunt. He was interested in the truth, not just in winning, and with him in charge I felt as though New Road had a chance of getting a fair deal.

But that didn't mean that he would just let us off the hook because I said we were innocent. Following the routine legal procedure, Rosner convened a grand jury to present the evidence Kukis had collected and see if they could make an indictment stick. He called fifteen New Road employees to testify as well as about twenty of our vendors, though we didn't know they'd been subpoenaed until they started calling me and asking—angrily, but rightfully so—just what was going on in our schools.

"Talk to our lawyers," was all I could tell them. "Here, I'll give you their numbers."

Kukis targeted the vendors to, he hoped, support his charge that we were making large end-of-year purchases to zero out our accounts and avoid sending any non-used money back to the state. Somehow, to him—and to Pamela Hall, who had brought this to his attention in the first place—this meant that New Road was cheating the state out of money. To everyone else, this was an innocuous, practical spending method and we certainly weren't the only state-funded company to engage in it.

But by the time the grand jury rolled around, there was a little more to it than that. While rooting through every piece of paper in New Road's office Kukis also had come upon some invoices he hadn't liked—the ones that itemized large purchases to keep them under $2,000. I've explained this before: it was a simple accounting practice that had been given the stamp of approval by our accountants, our auditors and even the state; at least, no one had ever told us it was wrong. For some reason, though, it stuck in Kukis' craw, and he was trying his best to somehow make a crime out of it. And he hoped that our vendors would back him up on it.

Pamela Hall was called before the grand jury as well, but those records are sealed, so I have no idea what her testimony was—I just know that it couldn't have been that convincing, because there was no indictment at the end of the testimony ordeal. No evidence of wrong-doing had been presented. There *was* no evidence, period. And with that, the grand jury simply disappeared.

And so did our old friend Pamela Hall—at least for a little while.

"Thanks for driving, Mark," I said as I closed the passenger door of his car. On the other side of the vehicle he was putting on his jacket, a look of sheer annoyance on his face.

"No problem," he answered flatly, then clicked the remote button on his car key. A double chirp signaled that the doors had been secured.

Walking silently across the small parking lot toward the front door of the law firm of Lomurro, Davison, Eastman and Munoz, I doubled my steps to keep up with Mark, trying not to think how out of place this all felt. Mark and I often went to outside consultants together, but in this context—with one of his ex-employees trying to extol revenge on him personally and on the entire company—I was a little bit afraid of his potential wrath. I hoped that he could keep it in check for this occasion.

"Good afternoon," said the receptionist once we were inside. "Are you here for the deposition?"

It had been ten months since the grand jury inquiries and in that time, things had grown pretty quiet. After failing to secure an indict-ment, Rosner had backed off the case—or, more importantly, had called Kukis off it. There had been no more interviewing, no further requests for documents and evidence. Rob Kipnees, I imagined, had gratefully gone back to his regular legal work and put New Road on the back burner, where it belonged.

And, most importantly, our schools had continued to thrive. None the wiser to anything that had happened, our students had gone on with their lives, had learned and grown and reached for more than they'd ever thought possible. I finally felt like I was getting back to where I was supposed to be.

And, of course, that was when I was thrown another curveball.

Pamela Hall filed a civil suit against New Road, Mark, Dave and myself. She said that we'd created a hostile work environment and forced her to commit illegal acts while working for us. Our wrongdoing, she claimed, had forced her to leave her job. And of course, she wanted a lot of money in compensation for it.

"Yes, we are," I told the receptionist with a friendly smile. Underneath, I was probably just as angry as Mark was, but unlike him, I was good at keeping it hidden. Acting out in frustration would have gotten me nowhere, would have done nothing but make me look bad, and this wasn't the place for that.

The receptionist showed us into the deposition room, where everything was already set up. There was a table and some chairs on either side of it, a woman operating a video camera and a reporter with her little typing machine. On one side sat Robert Fettweiss, New Road's attorney in this matter; on the other was Andrew McDonald, who represented Hall.

And next to him was the plaintiff herself. She didn't even bother looking up at us. In fact, I'd say she purposely avoided it.

"Ellyn, Mark," Robert said, rising from his chair and coming over to shake our hands. "Just on time. We'll be starting in a minute."

He ushered us over to a couple of chairs next to his and we sat ourselves down, and for the first time since she'd quit her job at New Road in March 2004, I got a good look at the woman who used to be our controller. She wore a blue blouse under a black and blue tweed jacket; her straight-brown hair, cut into a bob, was sprayed into a solid puff around her face. She looked tired. It was no surprise to me when, early on in her testimony, she admitted that she'd taken some Xanax before arriving at the lawyers' office.

She'd turned up that day with a handful of papers, some notes on what she claimed could "demonstrate the level of professionalism" in the New Road office, but could not give a good reason why she had not turned them over to her lawyer at some earlier date—other than that she hadn't wanted to "inundate him with too much information." She and Robert Fettweiss, who would be conducting her direct examination, went back and forth about that for a while. In the process, she also revealed that she had struck a deal with the attorney general's office: She would be immune to prosecution in exchange for her testimony against New Road in the state's case against us. According to her lawyer, if she agreed to this, she could sort of ride the state's coattails when it came to finding evidence against us, making her civil case much less expensive to pursue. Plus, if there was an ongoing criminal investigation, the attorneys representing the school officers would most likely prohibit them from being deposed in a civil case—potentially ensuring Pamela an easy victory.

All in all, Pamela Hall appeared to be just as lost that day as she had been when she had worked for us—and just as unwilling to take responsibility for her own actions or her lack thereof.

"I was so busy," she said about her early days at New Road. "I was working ten-hour days. I was working Saturdays, when nobody even knew I was there. And all I knew was that Mark was never happy with anything that I did, and I couldn't figure out why."

Did she ever think to ask? I wondered. Whenever I felt like someone was unhappy with my performance, I confronted them on it—if only so that I could remedy whatever I was doing wrong. That was the attitude I tried to instill in our employees; we didn't focus on recrimination but rather on making corrections and striving for improvement. If Pamela had been unwilling to understand that philosophy, then had there really been any chance for her to make it?

"You said you were failing in your job and did not know why. You stated that you were completely confused," said Fettweiss, referring back to one of her earlier statements. "Can you explain to me what you meant by that term?"

Pamela stuck out her bottom lip and exhaled sharply, blowing her curled-under bangs off her forehead. Her eyes roamed the ceiling for a moment as she tried to come up with the right words to say.

"Nothing made sense," she finally answered. "And I could tell they were not happy with my performance regardless of how hard I worked. All of the projects that I was given had unrealistic timetables.

Mark said I was not doing the work that he had hired me to do, and I explained that I couldn't do any more than I was doing. He precluded me from hiring additional staff, and I was so inundated… The accounting didn't make sense. The purchasing didn't make sense. The financial statements didn't make sense."

Was she listening to herself? Under the table, Mark kicked the side of his shoe against mine, and I looked over at him; I could tell that he was really holding himself back from bursting out screaming. Honestly, I wasn't too far behind him. I looked back at Pamela, sure that my face betrayed my incredulity.

None of the basic accounting work made sense, I wanted to say. *What kind of CPA are you?*

Pamela went on to outline how Mark demoted her after a while, citing a restructuring of the accounting department. That was accurate; that had really happened. What she seemed to fail to realize was that it had been because of her refusal or inability to do her job as the controller—not because Mark or anyone else simply had it in for her.

"He said, 'You are an excellent accountant,'" she reported, her voice flat, her demeanor aloof. "'But other than that, you are of no use to me, and you are not doing the job I hired you to do—supervise a department and implement procedures to ensure a well-oiled machine.'"

That was right; putting appropriate procedures and controls into place was the first entry in the job description we'd given her. The one she now claimed, during this deposition, that she'd never seen.

"Did you think you were doing a competent job prior to that?" Fettweiss asked.

"When I was given realistic timelines, which was very rare. And when I was given the information I needed to do a particular task. Then I felt that I had the ability to do a competent job. However, I felt like I was failing, and I could not understand why."

And there was the heart of it: Nothing was ever Pamela Hall's fault. Anything that she did wrong was simply the end result of the people around her and the circumstances to which she had been subjected. She was an unwitting player in her own life, it seemed. I wondered how she'd ever come up with the idea to sue us.

The deposition went on and on that morning; it seemed like it would never end. Fettweiss asked Pamela question after question about her employment at New Road, her job responsibilities and the people

she worked with—several of whom she identified as "less than honest" or as having grudges against her, though for no real specific (or
at least logical) reasons. She asserted that she supervised members of
the accounting staff but then later, when alleging their participation
in what she believed was shady bookkeeping, said that she was not
responsible for any of their actions, putting all that blame instead on
Mark. Even though she oversaw these people's work. Even though she
never mentioned any problems with them to Mark.

She outlined all the things that she thought that all of us at New
Road had done wrong—the end-of-year spending, the itemized invoicing, buying supplies and then putting them in storage instead of using
them right away. But, she did not offer one shred of explanation as to
why she did not alert anyone—including the auditors, with whom she
spent eighty hours (eight weeks for about ten hours per week, according to her own testimony)—about these supposedly improper actions
while she still worked there. While she was signing our checks for
purchases, while she was supervising the accounts payable bookkeepers and signing off on their entries, while she was watching what she
claimed was illegal activity going on all around her, she kept quiet. She
let "it"—what she said were criminal actions—happen.

"This wasn't a big secret, what they were doing," she commented,
her voice dripping with disgust. "A lot of people in the organization
witnessed it. It was not hidden. It was not kept quiet. It went on year
after year, and people were compensated handsomely for being loyal."

I sighed and put a hand up to my forehead for a moment. I just
could not believe what she was saying. These accusations—the idea that
anyone at New Road could have perpetuated a conspiracy of criminal
activity of the scope that Pamela Hall described—were just baffling to
me. They seemed like the ramblings of a paranoid, insecure woman,
and I couldn't believe they were getting any credence whatsoever—or
that I could be incriminated for being generous when it came to salary
scales and contingent-pay plans.

Perhaps the most infuriating point, however—and one that came
up several times

throughout the deposition—was that Pamela Hall had never even
really studied the New Jersey State business and finance regulations,
the rules to which New Road's accounting procedures were supposed
to adhere.

"Have you ever reviewed the New Jersey regulations governing the operation of private schools?" Fettweiss asked at one point.

Her answer: "Very briefly."

Later, he asked, "Based upon your review of the New Jersey Department of Education regulations, had you formed any opinion as to whether this year-end spending to which you have been alluding was appropriate under the regulations?"

Her answer: "I didn't review the regulations in any detail. I didn't study them."

"Did you feel an obligation as controller to independently review the regulations that govern the Department of Education rules for how private schools can spend their money?" Fettweiss countered.

Her reply was that she was responsible for all of our schools, many of which were not in New Jersey, and so her time was too "thinly spread" to dedicate to learning New Jersey's standards. However, New Jersey was the only regulated state—the only one that required adherence to published accounting regulations. All the other states we worked with called only for statements prepared according to the generally accepted accounting guidelines and had no hard-and-fast rules pertaining to allowable or non-allowable expenses.

A lame excuse, I thought, wishing I could jump in and say something to her, or at least ask her what she'd thought she was supposed to be doing in her job at New Road. Over and over she asserted that though she had been hired for a position of considerable authority in the company, she was not responsible for anything that happened during her employment, that she continued to overlook and even approve what she now deemed illegal practices because she feared for her job if she didn't. Instead, she "hoped and prayed" that the auditors would uncover our alleged wrongdoing while continuing to sign off on their annual reports, which never mentioned any of the issues she had with us.

"With regard to your failure to provide the auditors with any information and your concern that you would be fired," Fettweiss asked her, "did anyone tell you that was what would happen if you provided the information to the auditors?"

"No," Pamela admitted.

"Did Ellyn Lerner ever say to you, 'Be careful what you say to the auditors'?"

Her face twisted up in anger, Pamela barely parted her lips and uttered another "no."

"Did Dave, New Road's co-CEO, ever say that to you?"

"No."

"Did Mark, New Road's CFO, ever say that to you?"

"No."

I don't know how many times they went through that exact same exchange. Did she tell any of us about *any* of the improprieties she had supposedly discovered? No, no and no. Did she tell any of us about what she thought was the misallocation of a large purchase of computers for our office staff? No, no and no. Was anything concealed or hidden from the auditors so that they could not find these so-called improprieties if they were looking for them? No, no, and no. She just went on and on about how she couldn't believe that New Jersey would be okay about our spending most of our budget at year end, about rumors that she interpreted as true and about procedures that she interpreted wrongly—she presented them as actual state regulations, which, of course, she had never read. All of it was confabulation. She filled in gaps in her own knowledge or understanding with supposition and speculation.

Now, if Pamela had come to me and told me about any of this at the time, I could have made her a hero; she would have been heralded for protecting our schools from poor or improper controls and procedures. If she'd brought her concerns to my attention I would have either reassured her that we were doing nothing wrong and seen to it that she'd gotten the training she needed—especially about those regulations—or I would have asked her to implement controls that would have prevented any further wrong entries in the books. I never would have told her to hide information because there was nothing to hide, and I never would have stood for any of the misconduct she purported. That just was not the way that we did business. And if she thought it was, then she'd been an even worse match for New Road than I'd ever thought.

Eleven

That first day, the deposition went on until it was dark outside, at which point we agreed to reconvene at a later date. Outside the law firm's office, we all moved slowly to our cars, stiff and exhausted from being cooped up in that little room all day.

"Unbelievable, huh?" Mark asked me as he pulled out of the parking lot, aiming the car in the direction of the parkway.

"Hm," I replied, nodding my head tiredly. There were so many thoughts, so many emotions in my head after hearing all Pamela Hall had to say, I couldn't even form a coherent thought out of them. I never would have imagined that something like this would have happened to me. It wasn't that I was shocked by Pamela's civil suit—disgruntled ex-employees happened, that was just a fact of business—but that she would try to criminalize my life's work... It was so unbelievable to me that it almost didn't feel like it was real.

I closed my eyes and rested my forehead against the cool window. Neither of us said anything else for the rest of the ride home.

Two weeks later, Mark and I traveled again to Lomurro, Davison, Eastman and Munoz and were again shown into the little deposition room. Taking my seat, I threw a steely glance in Pamela Hall's direction, wondering what bombshells she would drop on us this time.

This session started out almost identically to the last, with Pamela acknowledging that she'd taken Xanax before her arrival. Upon further questioning from Fettweiss, who continued to conduct the direct examination, she denied that she'd ever given any of her pills away to coworkers at New Road, though Fettweiss had been told by several of our bookkeepers that Pamela had told her subordinates to take some of her Xanax whenever she'd given them stressful deadlines. She did admit that Mark had asked for ten of them, and she had politely obliged.

I looked over at him when I heard this, and he just shrugged his shoulders at me. Was that an admission on his part? Or a way of saying, "This lady's crazy. What on earth is she talking about?" I made a mental note to ask him about it later.

Fettweiss then asked Pamela to review some notes that she had previously submitted. In them, she'd written about an article she'd read concerning the proprietors of a school who had been sentenced to jail for giving their friends and family various no-show jobs. I imagined how her eyes must have lit up when she'd come across it; surely, it had given her some great ideas about what to charge us with.

"Now, does a no-show job, as you use the term," Fettweiss began, "mean that the employee doesn't show up for work?"

"Partially," Pamela replied, holding her chin high as if she were the authority on the subject.

"And when you say 'partially,' what do you mean by that?"

"It could be the person doesn't show up for work or is not being paid for the job that they are hired for."

I shook my head a little. That answer just didn't make sense. A no-show job meant that an employee was on paper only—he or she was paid, but did not actually perform the job. To suit her own needs, Pamela was putting a new definition on the term, one that I was pretty sure would not hold up in a court of law.

Still, Fettweiss entertained her.

"So in your view, there are two possible categories for no-show jobs, is that correct?"

Pamela tossed her hair and looked off to the side as if the subject bored her. "Correct."

"The first category is a person who is on the payroll but doesn't come to work, correct?"

"Correct."

"And the second is a person who is on the payroll and *does* come to work... Is that right?"

She nodded at him, as if this made complete sense to her. "Correct."

"But is hired for a different job than what he or she is performing?" He was giving her every chance here to back out of her mistake.

"Correct."

Fettweiss paused for a moment, looking down at his legal pad full of notes, his pen poised. He seemed to be formulating something in his head. "Would an example of that be someone who is hired as a controller but doesn't do that job? Is that the kind of thing you're thinking of?"

It was all I could do not to jump up out of my chair and start cheering.

Pamela glared at him for a moment. "No, it's not."

She then went on to say that though she hadn't been aware of anyone who had a no-show job at New Road, the attorney general's office had implied to her that there were several—all of which were news to me. So was the "fact" that Dave and I were both among the guilty. The reason she put me into this category?

"Well, she was paid about a hundred forty thousand dollars per year to be the executive director of New Road Schools in New Jersey while she was running twenty-six schools throughout the United States. Her salary from New Jersey was not justified by the amount of time that she spent on the New Road schools."

At that, I had to keep myself from laughing. This was so far-fetched. Me? A no-show? I spent practically every waking moment of my life at New Road, and New Jersey was the only state in which I was certified to be a school administrator and principal. Dave and I hired executive officers to run the schools in other states; really, I didn't get involved much with their day-to-day operations. I provided leadership to all of them and made sure that they all ran their operations according to the model that was developed and perfected in New Jersey. The funniest part was that I didn't even take the maximum allowable salary under the New Jersey regulations, which was about $196,000 at the time.

If Pamela had opened her eyes and looked around once in a while at New Road, she never would have made such a ridiculous claim to the attorney general. My New Jersey schools were obviously where my heart lay; they were also where my office was situated and where all my innovative practices were put to the test. I was always at the facilities, involved with the staff and students, the buildings and programs, on practically a daily basis. Yes, I did travel out of the state on occasion but only to make sure that the other schools were using the New Jersey model. And when I did, I kept careful track of the days I was not in New Jersey and adjusted my salary downward accordingly, taking much less than what would have been allowable.

Anyway, how could she have said that the work I did didn't justify my salary? When I thought about it, I was actually a little insulted.

"Did you mention that to anyone?" Fettweiss asked.

"I mentioned it to Mark."

"And what did you say to Mark? What did he say to you on this subject?"

"I said we're overcharging the state of New Jersey for Ellyn and Dave, and he said, 'No, we're not.'"

Because we weren't, I thought, sinking down into my chair. Her accusations were making me feel a little bitter.

"Is there a regulation governing the New Jersey private school system that discusses how salaries should be allocated?" Fettweiss went on.

"Not to my knowledge."

"Did you ever see such a regulation?"

"Not to my knowledge."

"Did you ever go look for such a regulation?"

"No, I didn't."

And there was Pamela Hall's entire defense, it seemed. Every time Fettweiss mentioned regulations, it was "not to my knowledge" and "no, I didn't." Did she report anything about Dave's and my salaries to the auditors? No, she didn't. Did she have a responsibility to do so, since she thought our pay was allocated wrongly? Not to her knowledge. Was she familiar with the New Jersey regulations regarding specific expenses that she deemed inappropriate? No.

For all her accusations against us, she sure didn't have much to back them up.

Instead, she consistently claimed that she couldn't remember anything, that she didn't know anything, that nothing was her fault. She even claimed ignorance of the accepted ethical standards governing all

CPAs—something that should have been at the forefront of her mind at all times.

"Would it refresh your recollection if I were to tell you that there is a standard that requires you to resign your job rather than sign a material false document?" Fettweiss pressed.

Of course, her reply was: "I don't recall that."

She also couldn't recall ever having read the generally accepted accounting principles pertaining to start-up expenses—the one-time expenditures to put a new facility into operation. Or explain exactly why she believed that Mark's refusal to hire her an assistant—to do the work, I imagined, she herself didn't want to do—was driven by some sort of interoffice conspiracy wherein we committed fraud, falsified accounting records, paid people *not* to show up for work, and made Pamela Hall's life hell because she was the one beacon of truth and integrity in the entire affair.

Sure, I thought. *That makes perfect sense.*

Next, Fettweiss gave her a document to look at—New Road's financial analysis for 2003. Packet of papers in hand, he held it up and pointed to a particular page, then asked her what was on it.

"It shows where they were projecting how much money they needed to spend in order to spend up to the tuition rate so they didn't have to send the money back to the school districts," she replied.

I rolled my eyes. That had not been our intention in the least. We didn't just go out and buy things so that we wouldn't have to return money to the state, as if we were trying to cheat it out of its own money. On the contrary, that money belonged to New Road and we used it to buy the things that New Road needed. How could it be a crime to spend the money that the state allotted for use by the students?

"Ms. Hall," Fettweiss asked, "did you ever read any of the New Jersey Department of Education regulations dealing with the issue of year-end spending?"

"No, I did not."

"So, what made you feel it was inappropriate, if you didn't look at the regulations?"

For this issue, he asked that she look only at one of our expenditures: the eye lab facility in our new Somerset school, wherein we trained our students to become ophthalmology assistants or to work in commercial eye labs. Sure, we'd done a lot of purchasing for that area before the school opened; it was brand new, barely had anything but a few cabinets in it. We needed furniture, tools and eye-exam equipment, and that stuff did not come cheap.

"During the 2002 audit," Pamela began, "I overheard a conversation between Mark and the partner in charge of the audit talking about fourth-quarter spending and how purchases made in the fourth quarter could possibly be capitalized as inventory and not expensed in the current year."

"Did you draw from that conversation that the external auditor was aware of the existence of this issue?"

"That was during the prior year, and I don't know what was contained in the prior year's financial statements."

"And you never went back to look at them, correct?"

"I prepared them."

I shook my head. Had I heard her correctly? She'd prepared them, but she didn't know what was in them?

She really needs to lay off the Xanax, I thought, looking at her out of the corner of my eye.

Pamela went on to claim that the eye lab had been on a financial statement the year prior to its introduction into our curriculum, and I could see where that might have given her pause, but in reality there was nothing wrong with this. We'd needed to set up the optical lab prior to offering the courses, of course. And how could that have been a crime—to set up a program with all of the materials prior to the program beginning? It certainly wasn't under the accounting procedures pertaining to start-up expenses.

In the end, she acknowledged that the auditor in question had never pushed the issue of the eye lab expenses any further, which meant that, really, there was nothing wrong with it. He could have told us to reclassify the transaction more appropriately, or he could have issued a qualifying opinion on it. He'd done neither. The only "evidence" that he'd even noticed the issue at all was this alleged conversation Pamela had supposedly overheard. Which was a flimsy so-called fact, to say the least.

Then came the *pièce de résistance*—the statement that made all of Pamela Hall's actions make sense, at least in her own mind. In response to Mr. Fettweiss' questioning about the immunity agreement that Pamela had struck with the attorney general's office, she exclaimed, "Look, I didn't want to start any trouble, but I knew that Mark was going to fire me as soon as he hired a new controller. He said he wouldn't—that he was leaving me in the position of senior staff accountant—but I didn't believe this to be true. And I was under such stress and working under highly unprofessional working conditions, so I consulted with a lawyer as to what my options were. I was told to go down to the AG's office, to protect myself."

Protect herself from what? I wondered, sitting up straight in my chair. This was getting interesting at last.

"After I was gone," she continued, "it would just be a matter of time until the new controller found all these mistakes and improprieties and that Mark, Ellyn and Dave would probably blame me. Then, I would be the one under scrutiny, and I had a license to protect."

So that was it! She'd known she was failing, that either controls were not being adhered to or regulations were being overlooked, and that she was to blame. So, she struck first in order to protect herself against any possible improprieties that would or could have been found after her departure. There was no more justification.

Feeling more discouraged than ever, I tuned Pamela out as she continued on about how she wasn't to blame, despite these admittances. I just couldn't listen to any more—my brain couldn't take it. Every answer she gave was more ludicrous than the last; nothing was her fault, she had no recollection, *ad infinitum.*

"She still has no idea what she's doing," Mark leaned over and whispered to me at one point, one hand cupped around his mouth.

I smirked, then raised my eyebrows and nodded in assent. "Sad but true," I mouthed. I couldn't imagine her ever winning this case—or ever presenting any real evidence to the attorney general. There was no way we could ever be prosecuted as criminals.

Twelve

As ridiculous as Pamela Hall's deposition was, the lawyers representing Dave, Mark and me would not let us testify to contest any of what she said. Keeping in mind the district attorney general's still-pending case against us, they didn't want us to be deposed because they didn't want any of our statements on record at that point. Not knowing what Rosner and Kukis had up their sleeves, I could understand the apprehension. I didn't want to give them any more fuel for their fire, either.

Partially because of this, our insurance company decided to offer Pamela a nominal monetary settlement. I was sure it wasn't what she wanted; it wasn't nearly as much as she'd asked for in the suit. I also didn't like that it was sort of akin to admitting our own guilt in the matter, though my attorney assured me it wasn't.

"It's just go-away money, Ellyn," he told me. "Pamela had no case, but her lawyer would have pushed it as far as he could anyway. And it would have cost you an awful lot in legal fees. The insurance company was cutting your losses."

That explanation was okay with me. I was ready to do whatever I had to in order to let it all go. It had been two and a half years since the raid on the New Road offices and no charges had been brought against us—nor would they, I thought, at that point. As I've said so many times before, we had done nothing wrong and besides, by then, I figured that statute of limitations had run out. Rosner hadn't been able to get a grand jury indictment, and Kukis wasn't finding any new evidence. With Pamela's civil trial out of the way, I felt like I could finally relax.

But, that was when the sleeping dog was awakened.

Probably angry that the insurance company—and her own lawyer, who had recommended this settlement—had so severely devalued her allegations, when her civil case was through, Pamela Hall did not just go away. Instead, she marched herself back over to the district attorney general's office and laid it all out for them—all the improprieties she felt had gone on at New Road, all the illegal stuff she claimed we were doing, everything she had said against us at her deposition. The thing was, she didn't have Fettweiss to rein her in there; she simply had the eager, wide-open ears of Detective Kukis.

But she didn't have our friend Andrew Rosner to listen to her—and too bad, because he might have put a stop to her. Rosner, I learned, had been transferred to another division, and a new deputy attorney general was named to the case.

"Are you *serious?*" I asked Bob Fettweiss when he told me this bit of news over the phone. I was in my office, making my monthly calls to the heads of our out-of-state schools. He'd caught me in a moment of downtime.

"Afraid I am." He sounded genuinely sorry to say it. I knew he had respect for Rosner, as did I; as the DAG assigned to our case, Rosner had had considerable discretion regarding the decision to bring this case forward or, hopefully, dismiss it. He also could have moved it to the civil or administrative law offices, where all of our attorneys believed it should have gone. At least he kept Kukis on a short leash, kept him honest, which probably saved us quite a bit of trouble.

"And this is off the record, Ellyn, but Andy was friends with some of the guys around here, and word is the whole case made him uneasy. I had lunch with him recently and he said that Kukis was relentless, always going to the higher-ups to push his case. Rosner was under a lot of pressure from above to move Kukis' case along, but it was difficult. His bosses ended up transferring him out."

Somehow, this didn't surprise me. I knew that at first, Rosner had thoroughly believed Kukis' theory about our case. However, I believe that when he saw that Kukis had no evidence of wrongdoing, and that in fact a preponderance of evidence showed that the schools had never taken their entire state-granted tuition rates, he began having doubts. Not so much about New Road, but about the Kukis' motive for pursuing such a weak case.

"How do you know that he was uneasy?" I leaned my elbows on

my desk, pressing the phone to my ear, my heart beating hard. A new deputy attorney general? Rosner admitting he had a problem with our case? These were not the updates I wanted to hear.

"Again, off the record, Ellyn."

"Of course, of course." I wanted to yell at him to get on with it already, but I held back. I understood his trepidation.

"Well, this is partly what Rosner said, partly what we've pieced together ourselves from our knowledge of the political agenda in Trenton. Seems the attorney general's office wants to make an example out of New Road—they want indictments and headlines, and they have Gregory Paw, head of the criminal justice division, backing them up. There's this US attorney named Chris Christie, who's just been torching criminal justice because of the prior AG, Peter Harvey. He was weak, and Christie wanted to bring him down. The division brought Paw in from outside New Jersey to beat Christie's federal conviction statistics here at the state level."

"So we're just a pawn in all this?" I asked. My eyes blankly searched my office, as if the potted plants or the filing cabinets could give me an answer. "Why would anyone have it in for us like that?"

"Who knows? Paw's got stars in his eyes. Wants to be famous. He's one of those muscle-men prosecutors, like Elliot Spitzer or Nifong. They get elected by touting their success in bringing down public corruption. Paw wants to help Governor Corzine and the AG get credit for bringing down special-ed funding corruption in New Jersey. Corzine has a task force looking at the costs of special-education and general-education funding in the state."

"I know. I wrote several letters to them and a position paper with recommendations for the current school-funding formula. In fact, I even got a call back from Corzine's deputy, telling me how informative and educational my paper was." I laughed, but there was nothing funny about this situation. I sat back again, the wheels in my mind turning like mad. "So, who's taking Rosner's place?"

"Bob Brass." I heard him sigh across the phone line. "I don't know a lot about him but from what I've seen so far, he's not as headstrong as Rosner. He might not be able to stand up to Kukis or his higher-ups. Starting now, the investigator might be telling the DAG what to do rather than the other way around."

My stomach sank. "That's a hell of an insight, Bob. Are you sure about this?"

Fettweiss sighed again. "Unfortunately, yes. I know Kukis from way back when I was in the US attorney's office. He was one of my investigators on an IRS case and he did exactly what he's doing now. There was no evidence, and I ended the investigation but he kept pursuing it. Relentlessly. When I found out about how persistent he was, I confronted him. He went above me and told my superiors that I'd dropped the ball on a very important case for which he had all this evidence. Luckily, my superiors sided with me and got Kukis out of my way and off the case. I'm just afraid that Brass won't be as strong as I was and won't tell Kukis and his superiors to back off—especially because this case lines up nicely with the political agenda of the attorney general's office."

Now, for the first time, I was petrified.

⸻

Though most deputy attorney generals have at least some desire to move up the ranks and fill their bosses' shoes at some point, Bob Brass' sights were set a little higher. I had it on good authority that he was lined up for a private-partnership job. From what I'd been told, the official offer was to be confirmed upon his closing a high-profile case.

"Assuming this rumor is accurate, what does it all mean?" I asked Bob Fettweiss over the speaker of my cell phone. I was driving home from another long day at the office; the phone was on my lap. I felt like I asked him this very naïve question every time I talked to him lately.

"It means that Brass could perceive this case as his ticket out of the department. Which means he might let Kukis call the shots. It was Kukis' big find, after all."

Pulling up to the back of a line of cars at a toll booth, I gripped the steering wheel. Ben Kukis had apparently hit a wall in his case against New Road a good two years earlier but had never given up; I wondered, as I often did, just what we'd done to get so far onto his bad side. "What's he going after now?"

"Same old stuff," my lawyer replied. "Still trying to nail you on the end-of-year spending and all that." There was a rustling of papers on the background; he cleared his throat. "And now it looks like he's real interested in the invoicing issue as well."

I sighed. How many times was that going to come back to bite me? Yes, I'd told everyone to itemize invoices into components equaling $2,000 or less. Yes, that directive ensured that all those purchases would be expensed as supplies instead of recorded as capital assets. But could anyone point out to me where in the regulations it said I couldn't do that? Or, more importantly, which *law* forbade me from breaking down larger-scale items into their individually ordered component parts?

"Do they really have a leg to stand on?" I asked, inching my car forward in the traffic. "Can we really be prosecuted for this?"

"Not in my book. But then I'm pretty sure I'm not on the same page as Brass or the attorney general's office. Kukis got the okay to investigate it further. I have a subpoena here for all sorts of additional records that they want from you."

Thirteen

"What do you mean they want more information?" Dave was just inside my office door, which he had slammed closed moments before. "What's the problem now? Did we staple something in the wrong order? Use black ink when it should have been blue?"

Standing behind my desk, I concentrated on flipping through the stack of manila folders Kathy had pulled for me. I didn't want to look at Dave, didn't want to feed into his quickly mounting rage.

"Well?" he all but screamed at me.

Looking up finally, I saw the fury in his bloodshot eyes. He looked like he hadn't slept well in weeks. Everything was getting on his nerves lately, that much had been obvious. But I often thought that his frustration was really anger at me.

"More files," I told him, not really feeling like going into the whole explanation. I was tired of it all, too. Though I kept my game face on at all times—the last thing I wanted to do was make anyone else worry as much as I did—inside, I was crumbling a little at a time. "Nothing new, just more files for what they're already looking at."

"And what *aren't* they looking at, Ellyn?" He moved forward into the office, stopping behind the guest chairs in front of my desk. He leaned over, gripping the back of one of them with his fingers, his knuckles turning white. "Is there anything you've done that they don't think is illegal?"

And there it was. Now I looked at him long and hard, my eyes boring a hole right into his brain.

"How *dare* you?" I said. When I get sensitive, I either cry or yell back and although I didn't want to get into it with Dave—not this way, not in anger—I couldn't help myself. When he drew first blood, I lashed out. I just couldn't take it anymore. These volatile fights were getting worse, as were the cursing and shouting; both his and my outbursts were increasing in frequency, frenzy and duration. Since his heart attack in 1998, he'd been afraid of stress, and I knew that he blamed me for the unbelievable amount of stress that was brought on all of us by this case.

"How dare you accuse me of being the bad guy here when you've done nothing but sit in your office and bury your head in your paperwork?" I barreled on. "I still go out to the schools three or four days a week. I interact with the students and work with the teachers like nothing is wrong at all because I don't want them to worry that their jobs and their educations are on the line!"

Pausing, I took a deep breath. This was my standard attack, telling him that I did all the work, and honestly I was tired of saying it. I truly wanted things to be better between us; we needed each other, especially given the pressure we were under from the investigation. Besides, we were such great friends, and we'd been business partners for over a decade. I liked to say that New Road was my baby, my life, but he'd been instrumental in our success and in our expansion to other states. He was the visionary; I just executed the vision.

Now, we were like the Beatles—we'd had a great, creative run and done a lot of fabulous things together, but we just couldn't see eye to eye anymore. I was no longer capable of speaking to Dave in a confident, calm, strong manner and the fear in my voice triggered his toxic assaults. Maybe the responsibility for the situation wasn't all mine, but I just felt that I had to do something to improve our communication. Considering the bleak alternatives—keeping things the same or escalating our fighting—I knew I had to try.

"Dave." I sat down and motioned for him to do the same. "Please."

At this point we were three years out from the raid on New Road, and we all were feeling the strain. Other than my lashing out at Dave once in a while, I kept a lot of it to myself; I didn't even share a lot of what was going on with my husband and daughters. I certainly didn't let any of the school directors or staff think that I was anything but ebullient and excited about the future of our schools and our work with our students. Friends and family were always there for me no matter what, at any time, and I knew that I could confide in them about anything. But often I didn't, just because I didn't want to burden them.

This was my career, these were my schools, and I felt that I was the only one who should worry about any of it.

In front of me, Dave did not sit down. He just leaned in further, his shoulders hunching and his face beginning to turn red. This was a posture I was getting used to; lately he'd seemed to be angry at everything. And not just at me—everyone in the office was fair game. Anyone who was late, anyone who missed a deadline, anyone who didn't refill the coffee pot got an earful they would never forget. The pressure was getting to him and he was showing it.

He brought a hand up to rub his eyes, and I could tell that he was calming down a little. When he spoke, he tried to sound consoling, but it came out as an accusation nonetheless.

"I know you're having problems, especially with so much of the stress of this case falling on your shoulders," he began. "I know you're worried that your staff, the directors and the teachers who have always adored you will find out that you made mistakes."

Despite my best intention to remain strong and confident, I felt cornered, and I began to lash out again, though I tried to keep my voice calm. "I didn't *do* anything. Nothing illegal, anyway, and the only reason I'm trying to keep the staff from finding out is because they don't need that sort of disruption. They need to focus on the kids, and the kids need to focus on their work. No one needs to worry about the investigation but us."

"Us," he repeated with a smirk. He released his grip on the chair and turned his back on me, wandering around the office as if in thought. He paused at the far wall and looked at the framed photos that hung there—class pictures, some old, some current. I kept them there just for times like these, when I needed a reminder of why I had to keep going.

"And what will happen to us," Dave continued, "when you've had enough of these problems and decide to run off and handle things your own way, by yourself? Or, worse, with Mark? You'll leave me out of everything, I know you will. You are a one-man show—you've always done what you wanted to and left me to clean up your mess." He turned around to look at me, and now his face was just tired. "I've got no clean-up left in me, Ellyn. This school could go bankrupt and you're operating as if nothing is wrong, as if nothing has changed, and all because you want to protect *your people.* You'll never change, and I can't go on like this."

Hearing those words aloud, I swallowed hard, a lump forming in my throat. So many times—alone in my office, driving out to a school, getting ready for bed at night—I had wrestled with all the possible scenarios that could have happened. I thought about what I would do if the case went to trial, if it completely went away, if it dragged on forever and New Road went bankrupt because of it. I knew that it could all go south at any moment. If the school were indicted, the state would have put us on conditional approval until the outcome, which could have taken years. We wouldn't have been able to accept any new students until there was a resolution and without new enrollment to replace our graduating students and those who were mainstreamed back to their local public schools every year, we would definitely have had to lay off staff and cut services—a sure death sentence at any school.

Even further, if the New Jersey schools declared bankruptcy, all the out-of-state schools would follow suit. They operated under separate companies, but with the common ownership, the cancer would have spread. We wouldn't have been able to salvage any of it.

The long and short of it was that a hundred different factors could have ruined not only everything I had worked for but my personal life as well. I had so much invested in these schools that if they went under, so did I.

"What do you want me to do, Dave?" I asked quietly, sincerely hoping that he would have a viable suggestion and not just some smarmy remark.

He turned back toward me, fixing me with his gaze. "Fire Mark," he said so evenly that I thought I'd misheard him.

"Excuse me?"

"Fire Mark," he repeated quickly. "This whole thing is his fault anyway, isn't it?"

I looked out the window, thinking carefully about how I wanted to answer that. Yes, Pamela Hall had been Mark's employee, so I could lay the current fiasco on him: If only he'd treated her better, maybe she wouldn't have become so vindictive.

But, maybe she would have, I told myself, as always trying to see both sides of the story. Pamela was unstable, desperate. Could I really blame her bad behavior on Mark's poor management?

"That won't solve anything now and you know it," I finally answered.

"Then you'll have to buy me out. I don't want to work here anymore. The entire legal strategy in the case is devised around you two, anyway—you two and your lawyers. No one considers me."

"Now, Dave, that's not entirely true," I began. Since the whole ordeal had begun he'd opted out of many of the most stressful activities, like attending Pamela Hall's deposition. And I'd been okay with that; I'd even thought that he'd been sort of grateful to me for taking all the stress on myself. I saw now that I'd been mistaken, that he wasn't thankful. He felt not just left out but obliterated. He'd become obsolete in his own company.

"I'm out, Ellyn," he said. His voice was sad. "I'm out." And then he crossed his arms and leaned back against the wall, indicating that this was his final word on the subject.

Fourteen

Pulling up to our lawyers' office on a sunny mid-morning in June 2008, I tried to keep my mind blank, tried to focus on the momentary task of finding a parking spot. In the passenger seat, Mark was twisted around, facing the back.

"I'm telling you, if he worked any slower, he'd start growing moss on his back," he said loudly. In the backseat, Dave wheezed with laughter, his eyes tearing.

"Enough, you guys," I said dourly as I turned off the car. They both glared at me as they unfastened their seatbelts. "Sorry," I said. "I just don't think either of you are very funny and, anyway, this isn't the time or place for it."

It had been over four years since the investigation had begun, and I had already completed the buyout transaction with Dave. He was still working as co-executive director of New Road Schools out of an office in the Somerset facility, away from the central office and the stress of this case. Although he was technically still a director of the organization, he was no longer an owner and therefore had no money of his own invested in the schools. He and Mark had actually been getting along much better since Dave had given up the stress and responsibility of ownership.

We walked from the car to the building in silence, which I felt was more fitting for the occasion than nasty jokes about our people. Early that morning, Rob Kipnees, my attorney, had called a meeting of our legal team, which scared me. The only news you get in person is bad news.

We went inside and checked in with the receptionist, and Rob was out there in a flash, shaking all our hands and hurrying us into a conference room where the rest of the attorneys—Bob Fettweiss, Joe

Hayden and Barry Evenchick, all attorneys for the schools; Mark's attorney; Dave's attorney; Mark Olinsky, Larry Horn, Wally Timpone, who represented our employees, and one other attorney I hadn't met before—were already seated. Given all this talent, each billable hour for this little soiree would cost us $6,500, and it was slated to last for three hours. No wonder I was just as afraid of bankruptcy as I was the possible outcomes of this investigation.

Everyone's here, I thought as I pulled a chair up to the table. *Another great sign.*

"So," Joe Hayden began, "after spending almost four years interviewing as witnesses over thirty-five New Road employees and twenty-three vendors, colleagues, real estate agents, architects and the directors of your other schools—or, in other words, everyone you've ever known—the Division of Criminal Justice has finally come to a decision about your case."

Joe was a bit of a grandstander, a real statesman, and I could tell that he was pleased with his strong opening statement.

"About friggin' time," Mark muttered, and I shot a look at him. His leadership, or lack thereof, was partially responsible for getting us into this mess, I thought, and the least he could have done was take it seriously.

Joe cleared his throat and glanced confidently towards the other lawyers, disregarding Mark's rude little outburst. None of them had ever known quite how to handle Mark's remarks, even something mild like this, but it didn't seem to slow Joe down at all. "Barry and I had a conversation with Brass yesterday and he said that the Division of Criminal Justice is getting ready to indict seven of your people. And the company."

Joe paused again for what seemed like a couple of days. Across the table from him, I clutched my stomach to keep it from jumping out of my body. Indict? Seven people and the company? *Based on insufficient evidence?* This didn't even make any sense to me.

"What does that mean?" I asked for what seemed like the millionth time in the last couple of years.

"Well, he feels he doesn't have enough evidence right now to convict anyone, but he has enough to indict these people and see how it all shakes out. He's certain that once he puts it all in motion, he'll get the evidence he needs to convict at least one person of some sort of wrongdoing."

The explanation hung there among us for an eternity, the words repeating in my head until they made sense. "Indict seven people? On what charges?" I asked slowly, purposely keeping my voice low and restrained.

"They vary," Kipnees interjected. "There are the issues with the invoicing, and the sending books to the out-of-state schools. And yes, Ellyn, because I know you'll ask, I made sure he was acutely aware that we have evidence that your policy pertained only to the shipping of old, obsolete, discontinued and disposable books and computers to the out-of-state schools. His response was—well, he said he'd let a jury to decide. On a positive note, if you want to call it that, he now realizes that the end-of-year spending was all proper and acceptable, so that's off the table. However, he does have some issues with the items that were received towards the end of the year and when they were placed into service."

"He can indict our people based on these issues?" I asked just to clarify.

"Not totally," Kipnees replied. "He's also looking at some of them for perjury, obstruction of justice, conspiracy and/or theft."

I put a hand up over my eyes and shook my head, wishing that the old "out of sight, out of mind" trick could really work here. "Anything else?" I muttered, hoping very much that there wasn't.

"As far as charges, no." Kipnees glanced at Fettweiss and Hayden. "But there is more."

"When I talked to Brass," Hayden continued, "he said to me that he was happy he'd toured the schools. He was impressed with the quality of all your wonderful, important programs and said that he would feel awful if his department had to do something that would end up hurting the schools or even closing them down. So, he's hopeful that someone will step forward and do the right thing. He must have used that phrase three times. He said that you're all smart people and you know what will happen if you fight these charges. He said that someone should be prepared to do the right thing to save the schools for the students and the teachers."

Mark snorted. "Well, that probably makes you feel a lot better, doesn't it, Ellyn? Better that Brass thinks our programs are great and wants a felony conviction than calls us mediocre and can't find any wrongdoing."

This was dark humor, but it was very true and I couldn't fault him for it. Mark really knew my thinking so well.

"So, what does *that* mean?" I asked.

"It means that if one person will step forward and take a plea," Joe replied, "then all the other employees *and* the schools will be off the hook." He looked at me intently, waiting for me to process this offer.

"Are you saying," I began slowly, spreading my hands out on the table, holding myself in place, "that he wants one of us to throw ourselves under the bus?"

Hayden held his hands out in front of him as if weighing the inquiry. "You could say that, yes. Unfortunately, the outcome he needs is directly proportional to the resources they put into the case—not necessarily to the evidence he has. And this case consumed a great deal of time and energy. Hell, going through your email alone must have taken them weeks—there were fifty-eight thousand messages in all. The Division of Criminal Justice needs some sort of positive resolution to justify their investigation. Brass told me that this case cannot end without someone taking the fall."

I nodded stoically. "Couldn't that be construed as prosecutorial misconduct?"

Rob Kipnees responded. "We're teetering on the borders of that here, but I don't think it would be a wise strategy to imply that to them. We don't want to stick a needle in the prosecutor's eye at this point. He could get much more vindictive as a result."

Finally Dave spoke. "Could he be bluffing? You know—shaking things up with you guys so that you would come back and tell us?"

"Yes," Joe said. "He could be. But is that a chance you're all ready to take? I get the impression that playing brinksmanship with the schools is not something any of you is willing to do."

"I would call their bluff," Dave immediately replied. "Let them go to trial with this. No jury will convict based on this nonsense. None of us got any personal financial gain out of it, and neither did the school. I say fight this all the way."

I was enraged by this cavalier vote. Did he care so little about the schools going bankrupt or closing? I guessed that such haughtiness—or maybe it was courage—could only have been demonstrated by a person who'd already gotten their investment out of the company and had nothing to lose.

But then, I told myself, *Be fair, now.* This was a horrible situation for all of us. I couldn't expect anyone to know how to react, not even myself. When I thought about it, I figured that Dave just didn't want to see me throwing myself and my reputation away. He was used to my being a fighter and was surprised that I would give up without giving it the fight of my life in court. He probably was sure I would win, but I didn't think I could afford to. The cost would be the complete devastation of the schools and, probably, my reputation, regardless of exoneration.

Besides, Joe Hayden was right. I had told both him and Rob before that if it came down to a forced choice between saving myself and saving the schools, I would do whatever it took to ensure that the schools would survive. Rob, of course, had been very unhappy with that decision.

But in that instant, I knew what I had to do.

If I took this plea deal—whatever it was, and at that point I just didn't care—I would save the schools and the seven people whose lives could have been ruined by Kukis' witch hunt. I would keep New Road out of bankruptcy and avoid paying even more monumental legal fees, including the cost of seven new lawyers to defend those who ended up indicted. We'd already racked up $1.6 million in bills since the onset of the investigation and we hadn't even filed any motions yet, nor had we ever appeared in court before a judge. The money had gone solely toward paying for expert witnesses, forensic accountants, regulatory compliance experts and programmatic evaluators, as well as for the time our lawyers spent in informal meetings with the investigators and prosecutors and interviewing our prior auditors.

Those bankruptcy bells were ringing in my ears again—this time more loudly than ever. I could see us having to shell out another $6 or $7 million at least if the indictments all went through and we had to go to trial. With no line of credit or any other source of financing—and especially if the schools were forced to close down, leaving us with no revenue—this would be impossible.

And then, there was the timing to consider. If there were to be a trial, it probably wouldn't even get underway until a year and a half to two years down the line. With four years of our lives already wasted on this nonsense, could any of us really deal with that much more? Personally, I wasn't sure I could. Looking back at Dave, I wasn't confident that he could make it through another hour. His hands were gripping the arms of his chair like he was afraid it would spin out of control. His face was flushed, his brow lowered. I was almost a little scared that he would have another heart attack right there and then.

"I'll take the plea," I told the lawyers, and each and every one of them sat forward in their seats. Maybe they hadn't expected any of us to give in so easily; maybe they'd been gearing up for an argument. Maybe they preferred to let the indictments go through. I didn't know, and I didn't care. All I could think about was how I had built New Road and nurtured it into being the absolute best private school in the state for students with disabilities. All I could think about was saving it now from destruction.

"Ellyn, let's talk about what this means first," Kipnees cautioned.

I folded my arms across my chest, resolute that this was the answer to everything. "Fine," I told him. "But it's not going to change my opinion."

He glanced at Joe Hayden and Bob Fettweiss, who nodded to him to go on. "Well, Brass said that whoever steps up and takes the plea takes responsibility for everything. They'll be sentenced for misconduct of a corporate official as a third-degree crime, and the state will not oppose a recommendation of ISP."

"ISP," I repeated. "What is that?"

"Intensive Supervision Program," Kipnees continued. "You'd have to serve sixty to ninety days in prison, then you'd be released into a sort of probationary program."

I nodded sedately, as if I were listening to a menu of what was for lunch and not the details of my own potential incarceration. In the back of my mind, I fought off the panic that was threatening to rise. I was actually considering taking a guilty plea that would come with a three-month prison term, just so I could save the schools, ruining my own reputation to keep New Road's intact. Could I really do it? I had to weigh the options very carefully

If I let the indictments go through, I'd be throwing seven innocent employees to the lions—that was, if the attorney general's office was not bluffing. But how could I take the chance? The potential indict-ments included people who were truly the best in the field of providing special-education services to very needy students; it also included sev-eral of our accounting staff, who, despite what Pamela Hall claimed, had done nothing wrong. On top of that, New Road as an organization would be indicted, and that would be the worst thing of all. It would be a death sentence for the company to which I had dedicated decades of my life. Anyone who believed that an indictment alone, much less a trial and a conviction, couldn't bring down an entire organization just had to look at Arthur Andersen. If I let this happen, even if the outcome was eventually favorable, New Road would undoubtedly go the same way. Service companies just do not survive indictments and trial by the media.

I laughed. Looking around at the expectant eyes of the lawyers and, surprisingly, Dave and Mark, I realized what was going on there. "King Solomon's test," I said, more to myself than to any of them. The attorney general's office and the Division of Criminal Justice were threatening to kill the baby to see who would save it.

Well, guess that makes me the real mother, I thought.

"I'll do it," I reiterated. And that was where my troubles truly began.

Fifteen

Just as it is with everything in the judicial system, my plea deal took months to work out. Simply saying that I would take it was only the first baby step; after that there were letters to be written, negotiations to be considered, charges to be formally brought. When I'd said "yes," I'd thought that I would finally be bringing an end to the ordeal. I didn't know that I was just opening a whole other can of worms.

While waiting for something to happen, I spent my time as usual—at work, at the schools, and enjoying my family and friends as much as possible. On one hand, I really felt like an enormous weight had been lifted off of my shoulders and everybody else's. Mark seemed a little more at ease; Dave, when I talked to him, sounded less tense; and everyone at the school who was involved appeared to be getting on with their lives. Standing in the hallway during a change of classes, or having lunch with my coworkers in the office, I often found myself pausing just to take in the moment, to appreciate the friendly smiles around me, all the miracles in my presence.

I did this for you, I thought. *For my students and my people and my schools. Because I know you are worth it.*

Now, I wasn't trying to be some sort of martyr. On the contrary, I was just trying to put an end to a very ugly chapter in New Road's history. That accepting the plea would change my life forever was definite; my twenty-five-year career would effectively come to an end, and my hard-won reputation would be decimated. In my weaker moments I cried about that and wished that there could be some other way. On my better days, I reminded myself that because of the choice I made, the mission of New Road would continue. I was sacrificing myself for the good of the whole, and I was okay with that. In fact, it made me happy.

However, while I waited for the plea deal to go through, I had an awful lot of time to think. And sometimes, I wondered if it really had to end like this.

There are two requirements for a criminal prosecution: *actus reus* (conduct) and *mens rea* (intent). In my case, I was guilty of one of these—conduct, because I did give the directive to break down invoices for purchases into components, which avoided the state regulation's $2,000 rule—but completely unaware of the other. I had no intention of doing anything underhanded, and had no idea that the violation of this regulation could or would result in criminal charges. There was also the fact that we had left $2.6 million worth of back bills on the table, a loss that New Road decided to absorb rather than charge the state for that allowable amount. This meant that the state of New Jersey actually owed New Road that large sum—but we never sought to collect it. If my intent had been to get money that the company was not entitled to, then wouldn't I have at least taken the money that it *was* entitled to?

Regardless of what I knew or didn't know or did or didn't do, a defendant must be accused of "knowingly and purposefully" violating a statute, and so that was what I had been charged with. However, if the violation itself is ambiguous—that is, not clearly cut and easily proven—then a thing called the rule of lenity comes into play. This states that if a criminal statute or regulation does not clearly outlaw certain conduct, a person cannot be penalized for allegedly violating it. The rule also requires a court to resolve statutory and regulatory ambiguities in favor of criminal defendants.

I learned about the rule of lenity—which is, by the way, a constitutional right—thanks to some research I did regarding the legalities of the Division of Criminal Justice's case against me. As I said, I had a lot of time and an awful lot to think about, and at some point I just got it in my head: Why was I standing for this? I had never given anything up without a fight in my life, so why was I so willing to let this man take away my livelihood, my reputation and everything for which I had worked so hard?

Sitting in the library one night, poring over legal texts that I hoped would give me some overlooked miracle I could use for my own defense, one question kept revolving in my brain: Why was New Road being charged with criminal activity for supposedly violating regulations that had no basis in the justice system anyway? The rules we followed came from the state's Department of Education. If we'd gone astray of their guidelines, I would have admitted it and done everything possible to make sure we never did it again. This had happened to us before, when auditors had found errors we had committed in one area or another. The procedure was: They told us about it, we changed our policies or whatever led to the mix-up in the first place, they checked again to make sure we were doing it right, and then they patted us on the head and sent us on our way.

So, what made this time different? Why had this regulation violation not been handled administratively? Why had it been treated as a criminal violation?

For starters, there was Pamela Hall. If she really had felt as though we had been disobeying state regulations, whether on purpose or by accident, why hadn't she told Mark, Dave or me? As she'd admitted in her deposition, she had not done that at all. Her next step, if she felt so inclined, should have been going to the state Department of Education to report us. Again, she did not take this initiative.

Instead, feeling disgruntled against Mark for being let go and drowning in a chaotic personal life, she went directly to the Department of Justice and told them that New Road was breaking the law. Not that we were not properly abiding by regulations; not that our interpretation of them seemed to be off. That we were criminals, conspirators and thieves, and that she could give the DA the evidence he needed to convict us—starting with the list of regulations she thought we were breaking.

And that was where the rule of lenity should have come in. Kukis and Rosner, the DAG at the time, could have looked at those regulations and seen that because of their wording, it was difficult to pin them down to one set interpretation. The way that I interpreted them could have (and apparently was) different from how Pamela Hall interpreted them, and her take could have been different from that of the person in the state department who had written them. Even Nick Magone, the forensic accountant we'd hired to go over the issues in this case several years earlier, had said that depreciation versus expensing was a very loose area, subject to tons of interpretive opinion based upon facts and circumstances.

The rule of lenity, then, is what makes the necessary distinction to determine whether or not a crime has actually been committed. It focuses in some part on the language of a statue or regulation: It must be specific enough to prevent arbitrary or discriminatory enforcement of its terms (*Kolender v. Lawson*). The rule of lenity also orders that any statutory or regulatory language be interpreted in the strictest or narrowest of all possible alternatives. This is part of the due-process right of fair notice, and it ensures that a person cannot be prosecuted for another person's interpretation of a statue rather than for violation of the statute itself.

Fair notice also says that statutes or regulations must *clearly* detail what activities they assess as crimes so that individuals have adequate notice of what conduct is expressly forbidden. They must also clearly state that violations of these rules will result in criminal prosecution and lay out step by step what criminal penalties will be imposed for failure to comply.

No such "fair warning" was ever made clear in the regulations we were accused of violating—meaning that in essence, there was no case.

I believe that had Ben Kukis, Bob Brass or the attorney general's office considered the rule of lenity and fair notice, they could have seen that the case had no strength and declined to prosecute. They could have taken one look at the regulations Pamela Hall said we were violating and seen that, really, we weren't.

First, as I've said before, these rules were vaguely worded and definitely open to interpretation; nowhere did they say specifically that we could not, for example, break down invoices in the way we had been doing. Moreover, they did not say, "If you do not strictly adhere to the regulations in this chapter, you will be criminally prosecuted"—something that, for example, the Sarbanes-Oxley Act or the IRS statutes clearly delineated.

So, under the rules of lenity and fair notice, the attorney general's office should not have been able to bring this charge against New Road—or anyone else, for that matter.

When I discovered this, it sort of blew my mind. Had no one, especially not the deputy attorney general, read these rules? Were they that unfamiliar with the law? Or did the power they wielded make it possible for them to ignore parts of the law with which they didn't agree?

When I thought about all of this, I was more furious than ever. In my opinion, the investigators and prosecutors involved in the New Road case were ignoring the rule of lenity, creating differing interpretations of the state educational regulations New Road followed and using their conclusions to create a high-profile case against me. From my perspective, they were using the regulations' ambiguity to their advantage, and I would be the one suffering because of it.

And then, I read some more, and it only got worse.

⟨⟨⟨≈⟩⟩⟩

One of Brass' biggest bones of contention with New Road was our policy of breaking down large purchases into their component parts on our invoices. He called this *structuring invoices*—a phrase that I'll get into a little bit later—and said it was a criminal activity that overrode the Department of Education's rule of declaring any equipment costing more than $2,000 as a capitalized asset.

As I've already mentioned, yes, we did this: To the maximum extent possible, whenever there was a choice, we itemized the components when ordering certain large-scale pieces of equipment. But, we did so with the full knowledge—and, I would say, the blessing—of our accountants and our auditors and even the auditors from the state. Everyone knew that this was going on; no one ever told us to stop it.

As a matter of fact, itemization was common procedure in our industry. I could have told the Department of Ed about at least ten other private schools for the disabled that broke purchases down into components in order to avoid the $2,000 rule.

Regardless, if invoice itemization had not been in concert with either the spirit or the letter of the state regulations, I would have expected our internal controller—Pamela Hall, who never complained about it once—or our external auditors, or perhaps both parties, to make adjustments accordingly, and we all would have heightened our awareness of the nature of the wrongdoing. We would have striven not to let it happen again.

To try to find some clarity on just what we had allegedly done, I looked to the exact regulation we were accused of violating: N.J.A.C 6A:23 4.4 (a) (3), which stated that "fixed asset expenditures of $2,000 or more shall be capitalized and depreciated using the straight line method and a useful life consistent with current federal tax law." What we were doing was taking any purchase over $2,000 and making it into a series of smaller purchases, and then expensing them instead of capitalizing. Did the regulation say we could do this? Not exactly. Nor did it exactly say that we couldn't.

The problem that I saw was that the regulation did not define what constituted a fixed asset, and so there was a certain level of ambiguity regarding the categorization of a school supply or a piece of educational equipment as such. It mentioned the item's "useful life," but what did that really mean? If a piece of educational equipment was experimental in nature and might or might not have been incorporated into the schools' services or curricula, was it useful? Should we really have considered it a fixed asset?

The regulation does say to look to federal tax law for further explanation, so I did, and it defined the useful life of a few exemplary assets—one I remember was a computer. However, it also talked about experimental equipment (section 174 of the IRS Code) or a piece of equipment used for "ordinary and necessary expenses" (section 162) arising from federal mandates imposing that a school such as ours implement a transition service curriculum for all students age fourteen and older. That brought even further ambiguity to the equation.

Since I didn't get a clear enough answer from all of that, I looked to the standard accounting definition of the term *fixed asset* and found it to be an item that has "a probable future benefit"—an ambiguous phrase if ever there was one. The definitions also noted that a fixed asset must contribute to future net cash inflows (straightforward enough) and have a useful life extending substantially beyond the year it is placed in service—though there was no definition of the terms *useful* or *substantially.*

To tell the truth, until this case, I'd thought that a fixed asset was one that was not moveable—meaning you couldn't take it with you if you moved to another location. That was how much knowledge I had about these issues. Yes, I did give everyone the directive to order nothing over $2,000 and to itemize all components on equipment purchases, just to make sure. But I really didn't even know the nature of what we were itemizing. The accountants and auditors had said it was okay to do it that way, so I had put the procedure into place. If I didn't know that what I was doing was wrong—and in fact didn't even clearly understand the language of the regulation—how could I be prosecuted for how I handled it?

To further complicate the issue, the standard definition of *fixed asset* noted that any property that did not meet the definition's vague requirements had to be treated as an expense. Now, I remembered that Nick Magone had addressed this issue in his report. Digging back through my files at the office, I found the printout of it and sat down at my desk, anxious to reread what he'd had to say.

Unfortunately, it didn't give me any more clarity on the definitions—but it did reinforce my belief that it all came down to a matter of interpretation.

On page five of Magone's report, I found this:

> For example, something that would otherwise be recorded as a fixed asset in one instance can appropriately be recorded as an expense if, based on the individual's understanding of the program, the item in question was purchased for experimental use. GAAP [generally accepted accounting principles] allows the expensing of research and development-type expenditures. It is my understanding, based on interviews, that some teachers viewed certain programs as experimental.

This was how I saw it as well. There was a great deal of ambiguity involved, in my mind, in regard to much of the equipment that we purchased for our schools. Sure, a machine used in a print shop was made for commercial use. But what if it was only used for student training? In an educational setting, it wasn't generating any income, and its useful life was highly in question: Would it be too difficult for the students to use? Would they be bored with it? Would it get destroyed from the everyday use? Would we have to discontinue its use due to safety issues?

Further, what about those programs that we instituted at the beginning of one school year only to discontinue them the next or, at the most, two years later? We'd had a lot of programs that had gone that way—plate glazing, ceramic-mug coating, mug imprinting, oil-paint reproduction facsimiles, auto detailing, small-motor servicing, and Lucite cutting and bending, to name a few. The equipment we'd bought for those programs had not promised to contribute any future income to New Road, nor had we known if they would truly be useful. So, should they have been expensed or capitalized?

What this section of Magone's report brought home to me was that the useful lives of many of the items we were accused of inappropriately expensing presented a significant degree of uncertainty. I could not understand why anyone in the attorney general's office would approach this without applying the rule of lenity—which, it seemed to me, was exactly what they had done. I wondered what sort of justice that was supposed to serve.

I did a lot of research into the invoice structuring charges against us and how the rules of lenity and fair notice applied to it. One of the best ways to make a legal case for oneself is to find the precedent already set by the court, and that means coming up with similar cases where the ruling was in the defendant's favor. I didn't have to search too far to find plenty of precedent in this area.

First I found *Ratzlaf v. United States,* a case involving the anti-structuring provision of the Bank Secrecy Act. Ratzlaf was a guy who tried to pay a gambling debt to a casino with $100,000 cash. The casino staff told him that any cash transaction in excess of $10,000 had to be reported to state and federal authorities (i.e., the tax people), but they could accept a cashier's check for the full amount and avoid this. The problem was that he would have to purchase the cashier's check from a bank, and all banks are required to report cash transactions in excess of $10,000.

So, the casino assisted Ratzlaf in going to several banks and purchasing a series of cashier's checks for less than $10,000 each. He paid off his debt—and then was charged with structuring transactions because he evaded the bank regulation of reporting large cash transactions.

When the Supreme Court ruled on this case, it focused on the charge that Ratzlaf willfully violated this regulation—which he did. He knew that he was making the smaller purchases to avoid having them reported, and he knew that this conduct was unlawful. If he didn't know, well, then, the statute he violated, the Bank Secrecy Act, clearly laid it out for him. The language of that act's anti-structuring provision defines the word "structuring" and gives fair notice that violation of the provision could lead to prosecution. So, Ratzlaf had no excuse—he was convicted, fined and sentenced to prison

But in the New Jersey Department of Education code under which New Road operated, there was no such definition. It never even mentioned *structuring*, nor did it say that if we structured anything, we would be brought up on criminal charges. In contrast to *Ratzlaf*, wherein there was a code that clearly defined what would happen if someone disregarded it, we were given no notification that what we were doing was criminal—because it wasn't.

The next case I found was *Posters 'n' Things, Ltd. v. United States*, which involved a retail outlet allegedly selling drug paraphernalia. In its ruling, the Court held that the government had to prove that the defendant acted "with knowledge that the proscribed effects would most likely follow." That was, the government had to establish that the defendant knew that the items would likely be used with illegal drugs, which is, of course, against the law.

Similarly, in New Road's case, the attorney general's office should have had the burden of proving that we had structured our invoices *with the intention to commit a crime,* not just that we did it to avoid the state's purchasing regulations. How the prosecution would have proven this, I have no idea—another reason why I believe he pushed for the plea bargain.

When I was through with my legal research, I had an enormous amount of precedent on my side. I also had the rule of lenity, the fair notice concept and, I found, the *void for vagueness* doctrine. Derived from the due process clause of the fifth and fourteenth amendments, it requires criminal laws to be written in language that an average person can understand and specifically detail the procedures that must be followed by officers of the law regarding violation of the statute in question.

One of the most frequently cited cases when the void for vagueness doctrine is used is *Connally v. General Construction Co.*, wherein Justice Southerland pronounced that "any statute which either forbids or requires the doing of an act in terms so vague that men of common intelligence must necessarily guess at its meaning and differ as to its application violates the first essential of due process of law."

Extrapolating this to the New Road case was simple: The state regulation regarding invoicing, capitalization and expensing was vague. It did not lay out in plain terms that if the rule was not followed to the letter, any transgressors would be prosecuted. Nor did it say what any such punishments would be.

And I found so many other cases that reiterated this sentiment. *Lanzetta v. New Jersey. Watkins v. United States. Raley v. Ohio.* There was ample explanation of and support for the void for vagueness doctrine, and I was sure that it would apply in my case as well. Over and over, everything I read said that it did.

Unfortunately, however, it's not enough to challenge a law solely on the basis of imprecise or unclear wording. Yes, the state regulation in question was vague. But did that excuse me from violating it? Did it mean that I hadn't committed a crime?

To answer such questions—and to challenge the law—I had to consider some other questions:

- Should a layman such as myself have known that the conduct in question (*structuring* the invoices or breaking down large-scale purchases into their component parts) was so wrong that it was likely to carry a criminal penalty?
- Could the statute in question—N.J.A.C 6A:23 4.4 (a) (3)—have been worded more precisely, with clearer definitions? Should it have specified that structuring purchases to evade the Department of Education's regulation requiring the capitalization of fixed assets would have been a violation of law?
- Were there other statutes or regulations that were worded more clearly, or that contained better definitions, that would have made this regulation clearer for me?

The answer to the first one was simple: If I had known that violating the code would have led to prosecution, do you think I would have ordered the invoices to be done that way? For the second question, the answer is, "of course." There were over twenty-five definitions in the Department of Education's business and finance code but not one of the word *structuring* or the phrase *fixed asset.*

As for the third question, I looked at *Sabetti v. Dipaolo,* a case from 1994 in which the court held that a criminal statute fails to provide fair notice if a "person of ordinary intelligence…examining only the language of the statute…would be in some way surprised that it prohibited the conduct in question." To say that I was surprised that New Road had been charged with a criminal act for the way that we invoiced would have been the understatement of the century.

Besides, as *Sabetti* also showed, it's not enough for another text to elucidate the meaning of a law, code or statute. If the regulation in question was not clear enough, legally I did not have to look to another statute to make it make sense for me.

One last case that I looked at placed a little bit of a different light on the subject: *United States v. Eaton,* which involved a federal criminal prosecution under the Oleomargarine Act, a statute designed to protect the dairy industry from competition from a new product. Of course, that had nothing to do with my case, but what *was* relevant was *US v. Eaton*'s main question: Could a wholesale dealer in oleomargarine be held criminally liable for failure to conform to a regulation—keeping books and making returns—promulgated by the commissioner of Internal Revenue? That was, could he be criminally prosecuted for neglecting to follow a *regulation?*

In this case, the Court said "no." Relying on the rule of lenity and on the specific fact that the legislature did not, in the Oleomargarine Act, give Internal Revenue the specific authority to prosecute violations, the Court said that the prosecution violated the principle that "a sufficient statutory authority should exist for declaring any act or omission a criminal offense"—that was Congress' job. Congress had made it a criminal offense to neglect to do anything required by law in Section 18 of the Oleomargarine Act, but it had not expressly made it a criminal offense to neglect to do a thing required only by a *regulation.*

In the end, what *Eaton* established was the distinction that Congress could not delegate to any agency the authority to pronounce regulations that carried criminal penalties without explicitly iden-tifying them as such, as well as what the penalties would be. Again, for about the thousandth time, none of the Department of Education regulations New Road allegedly violated did this. And so, the Depart-ment of Ed had no recourse to criminally prosecute us.

After reading this last case, I closed my notebook, where I'd been furiously scribbling case numbers and explanations for months. I had hours and hours of work there, pages and pages of notes, all saying the same exact thing: The regulation in question was not worded clearly, the regulation did not say I could be criminally prosecuted, the regula-tion did not provide for any punishment for transgressions whatsoever. Add that to the fact that there was zero monetary gain for anyone—not me, not Dave or Mark, not any of the schools—as a result of the invoice *structuring* and it was crystal clear that no crime had been committed. Misconduct or a code violation, maybe. But nothing that should have been subject to criminal prosecution.

What was clear was that the attorney general's office was muscling a plea by threatening to ruin the school and many of its innocent employees.

What was also clear was that I would not stand for any of this.

Sixteen

"There's no way they can prosecute me," I said, sliding my folder full of papers across the table to Robert Kipnees. "Look, I have all this evidence that no crime was even committed!"

Taking the folder from me, he sat back in his chair and put it on his lap. He opened it up and flipped through a few of the pages, reading my notes, which I'd typed up neatly for him. I watched him expectantly—but then just couldn't wait for his answer.

"What do you think?" I asked, my voice almost a whisper.

He put the folder back on the table in front of him but left it open. "Well, we've discussed a lot of this already," he said, looking at me and raising his eyebrows. "And you're right. About all of it. This does support the fact that no crime was committed, either by you or by New Road."

I smiled and clapped my hands together. "Yes!" I shouted, feeling vindicated. "Yes!"

On the other side of the table, Rob was noticeably silent. My glee fading, I put my hands down in my lap.

"What is it?" I asked him, dreading his answer. "I mean... We take this to the AG and that's it, right? Brass can't indict me or New Road, and the whole thing goes away."

He shook his head then—not exactly the reaction I'd been expecting. "It doesn't work that way, Ellyn," he said. Arching his hand over the papers, he touched them with his fingertips. "This is excellent work on your part." He laughed a little. "If you ever want to switch careers, I'd hire you as an assistant without a doubt. But all of this is *defense*. Do you see what I'm saying?"

I thought about it for a moment. "No, not really."

"I'm saying that you can't defend yourself against *alleged* charges,

121

Ellyn. You can only defend yourself against an actual indictment, not the *threat* of one."

I sat back again and let that sink in for a minute. "So, you're saying that to use any of this evidence," I began slowly, "we would have to go to trial?"

"Yes." He nodded. I nodded back. "The research would form the basis for an appeal to the indictment. Granted, an appeal like that is hardly ever won. But you've got a useful defense here, and I think it could work."

Since the moment I'd agreed to take the plea deal, I had never once considered reneging on it. I wanted to do it; I had to do it to save the schools. This was the mantra I'd adopted, the mission on which I'd planned all along to follow through. But if the only way to make use of all this research I had done, the only way I could invoke my own constitutional rights, was to allow myself to be indicted—along with seven other innocent people and the schools—then how could I not consider it as an option?

"So, what if we did? What if we went to trial?"

Sitting forward again, Rob folded his hands on the table. "Well, in theory, you would win. In my thirty years of practice I have never been more sure that I could get an acquittal for a client. I just don't believe that a jury would ever convict based upon the evidence the DAG says he has, especially given all of *our* evidence." He pointed again to the folder. "All the other attorneys on the case agree with me as well. In fact, we're so sure that I would even waive your right to a jury if we did go to trial—and that's something I have never recommended to a client. The law is *so much* on your side, I would allow just a judge to hear the facts of the case and render a decision."

He paused, again looking down at the folder. "That being said," he went on slowly, "I *cannot* guarantee you that if we go to trial, the schools will remain intact. I've told you from the beginning that *you* are my client, Ellyn, and I only care about what happens to *you*. But you've made it clear that if I care about *you*, I care about *your schools* as well. With that in mind, I'm telling you now, I believe that the indictments would be the death knell for your institution."

I sighed. This was not news to me, but it also was not what I wanted to hear at that moment.

"Remember Arthur Andersen?" Rob went on. I nodded my head. We'd talked about that company extensively in comparison to the New Road case. "No company like yours, where your success is based on your word and your credibility—"

"And our standing with the government," I interjected.

"Yes," he agreed. "If those three things are demolished, then how will New Road survive? Very few service companies—maybe none—have made it through an indictment. Are you willing to put New Road through that test to prove yourself innocent?" He sat back in his chair, finished with his speech. But then he added, "If you are, I would be honored to represent your interests in the courtroom. But the choice is ultimately up to you."

I looked out the window of his office for a moment while I tried to gather my thoughts. All along I'd been so sure about sacrificing myself for New Road. But, now that I had all this new information, all this proof that I'd committed no crime, all this evidence that ensured that I couldn't be convicted… Was I willing to change my mind? Could I afford to win in this situation if it meant hurting so many others and selling the solvency of the school right down the river? That was the question that kept coming up for me—not just on this day but throughout the entire ordeal.

Sighing, I looked back at my lawyer. "You know, we had Howard Margolis come in and give us an expert opinion on New Road's operations." Dr. Margolis was an educational expert, a professor of educational and community programs at City University of New York, Queens College, and chairman of the special education department there. "He said in his report that our schools are among the best he's seen in his forty-two-year career in special education. Shouldn't the fact that we have a quality program—an *excellent* program, among the best in the state—shouldn't that all count for something?"

Rob nodded again. "Yes, it should. You've put an awful lot of work into those schools, Ellyn, and they are phenomenal. But if you ask me to fight to prove your innocence, I can't guarantee that the schools will continue to exist. I want to be very clear about that before you make your decision."

"It would be way too risky," I agreed, nodding as well. "It would be a shame for the students, for my staff and for me. It's more than my baby—it's an organism all on its own, a living entity. And, it's my sole retirement plan. I've always banked on having this valuable organization to sell when I'm ready to stop working. What will I do if it no longer exists? How will I pay back my loans, the mortgages, my promissory notes to Dave, all the business debt we had to take on just to stay alive? How would I even be able to continue to pay my legal bills?"

———

"Mrs. Lerner." At the bench, the judge adjusted his reading glasses and looked down at his docket. "Are you ready to proceed?"

It was a sunny Wednesday morning, six full months after the initial meeting with the lawyers, when Dave, Mark and I had learned about Bob Brass' ultimatum. In that time, I had gone through the entire range of human emotion: anger at Pamela Hall, hatred for Kukis and Brass, disdain for the attorney general's office, sadness about the potential ruination of New Road, elation over my own ability to save it. I had spent days crying over the whole thing and other days feeling invincible, like there was no way that any of it would affect me, the schools or the other involved employees. Agreeing to the plea deal that day had brought me a modicum of peace—but it had also left me with so many unanswered questions.

And then, I had come upon all that legal information, and everything had seemed so incredibly clear. With all that in my hands, I had felt *for sure* that there was a light at the end of this tunnel, and that it was not a train coming to demolish us all. Reading about all those precedents, all those other cases that had proven for us that while we might have violated a regulation, we had done nothing criminally wrong, I had felt so confident that I could—that New Road could—come out on top in all this.

And then, Robert Kipnees told me that the defense was worthless unless I was willing to go to trial and present it. And that meant throwing New Road under the bus. It meant taking those seven employees along for the ride with me, without being able to guarantee them a positive outcome. It meant putting all of us through probably several more years of legal wrangling and all the stress, frustration and financial obligation that would entail. And then, everything seemed horribly confusing once again.

So, in the end, I was back to making my own decision, relying on myself to find the best path to follow. I had to ask myself: Could I forfeit the schools and several of my people just to prove myself innocent? Could I call Brass' bluff and assume that the attorney general's office wouldn't really indict, that he was just saying he would to get me to take the plea in the first place? Or could I take one for the team, accept the plea deal, and put an end to the terrible ordeal New Road and its employees had suffered through for four years already—as well as my career and reputation?

In the end, I decided that, yes, I could. I could do that, and I would.

"Yes, Your Honor," I replied, standing up behind the defense table in the courtroom. I held my head high; I spoke calmly and firmly. "I'm ready to sign the plea agreement."

Seventeen

That night, I slept like a baby. Or, at least, better than I had in many, many months. Once I'd gone to court and officially accepted the plea agreement, once I'd gone ahead and gotten the ball rolling to bring this whole nightmarish chapter of New Road's history to an end, the weight that had been crushing my shoulders was suddenly released. Though I was digging myself into a hole—giving up my career, my reputation, everything I'd worked for in the last twenty-plus years, and earning myself a $50,000 fine and some jail time to boot—I felt freer than I had in a long time. I finally felt like something good really could come out of all this.

The next morning, because I wasn't sure exactly how I should have been acting, I woke up as I usually did and went about my normal routine as if it were just another day. I showered, dressed, made some coffee, checked my email. Then, I Googled my name to see what the news sites were saying about the hearing.

Now, my attorneys and I had spent a good deal of time crafting a press release about my plea agreement. We'd agonized over the details to include and the very specific wording to use, and this was what we'd come up with:

Ellyn Lerner Settlement with New Jersey State Court

On June 2, 2008, Ellyn Lerner, the founder and former officer of New Road Schools of New Jersey, Inc. (formerly High Road Schools of New Jersey, Inc.), entered a plea to a corporate misconduct charge in New Jersey State Court related to certain accounting practices in the schools' business office that occurred during the 2001-2002 and 2002-2003 school years. Ellyn Lerner elected to resolve this State of New Jersey investigation, which commenced over 4½ years ago in April 2004. Based on the agreement with the State, the New Road Schools, which were not charged, will be subject to a Monitor Agreement until such time as the Department of Education accepts the 2008-2009 fiscal year report (which usually would take place in or about November of the following school year, i.e., November 2009).

The violation to which Ellyn Lerner pled guilty involved her directions relating to the purchasing and itemizing of equipment and supplies to render each component under $2,000, the New Jersey statutory threshold delineating a capital item. New Jersey's Administrative Code (N.J.A.C. 6A: 23 - 4.4 [a] [3]) includes a citation stating that "a fixed asset over $2,000 be recorded as an asset and capitalized and depreciated over the life of the asset." The avoidance of this threshold, by breaking down a large-scale purchase into its individual components, was the factual basis for the criminal offense of corporate misconduct. The result of this misconduct had the effect of overstating tuition the year that the equipment was purchased. However, it also had the effect of understating tuition in the following four years. Over a five-year period, the net effect of the two accounting treatments (expensing or capitalizing) is zero. In 2004, the New Jersey corporation reimbursed/credited an amount of $914,223 from its 3 schools, to the New Jersey Department of Education related to this matter.

In the final case resolution, the State of New Jersey included a $250,000 restitution payment for settlement of a separate, non-criminal allegation. The New Jersey corporation, in the 2001-2002 and 2002-2003 school years, had the policy of shipping used, obsolete, or discontinued books and equipment out to the other schools whenever they were no longer in use. As no allocation had been made for the value of the books and equipment sent out to other schools, the State of New Jersey required restitution in this amount in order to resolve this dispute. This policy has completely stopped since after the 2002-2003 school year and unauthorized disposal or transfer of discontinued, obsolete or old materials is strictly prohibited.

These violations occurred partly due to gaps in internal accounting controls over five years ago, which have since been corrected with the implementation of appropriate and comprehensive controls and procedures. Ellyn Lerner has completely divested herself of all affiliation, employment with, and ownership of the New Road Schools. The New Road Schools are now owned by the employees of the schools under the employees' stock option plan.

Unfortunately, none of the news outlets to which my lawyers sent it printed a word of it. Instead, all the local media printed the press release from the attorney general's office. "Head of Private Education Services Corporation Pleads Guilty to Fraudulently Overbilling School Districts $1.3 Million," said its headline. When I saw it large as life across my computer screen, my stomach just dropped down to my feet.

"That's not my plea!" I shrieked, though there was no one there to hear me. "I pled to misconduct by a corporate official, not *fraud!*"

In fact, my lawyers had just spent over six months—and New Road and I had spent hundreds of thousands of dollars—making sure that this one little word didn't appear anywhere in the plea agreement or the monitor agreement. I hadn't committed fraud; I wasn't going to cop to fraud; and I certainly didn't want the stigma that went along with an accusation of fraud, no matter how unfounded or blatantly untrue it was. A word like that sticks around—it stands out in people's minds and can brand a person or corporation for life.

So, was this press release the result of an oversight by my lawyers? Had we missed a mention of fraud somewhere in the plea agreement? Or was this simply regular protocol for the state's attorney general?

Bob Brass had stood before four lawyers—Rob Kipnees, Joe Hayden, Barry Evenchick and Bob Fettweiss—and agreed that the word "fraud" would not appear anywhere in my plea or the monitor agreement. Now, his office was issuing statements like this press release, which used the word "fraudulently" five times. It also discussed New Road's out-of-state shipments of used books and computers; those were outside of my plea agreement and not in line with my allocution, which clearly said that I had no knowledge of anything but discontinued books or computers being either scrapped or shipped. I hadn't pled guilty to any of that.

I wondered what the word of a prosecutor really was worth. In my opinion, not very much.

"We will vigorously prosecute such cases to ensure that our education dollars benefit students, not corrupt corporate operators," Attorney General Anne Milgram was quoted as saying, and as I read it, I felt the ground give way underneath me. Things were not going to be okay; I wasn't going to get over this. I could take the legal battle, I could take going to court, I could take the plea agreement and I would even manage to get through the jail time. I wasn't going to be debarred and my teaching license would remain intact, so I even allowed myself once in a while to have hope that I would be able to return to New Road one day.

However, once the media did this—once I was labeled corrupt and guilty of fraud—I knew that any hope I'd had left was lost. Suddenly, things seemed very, very real.

I spent a good part of the morning reading through other Web sites that covered the hearing for my plea agreement. Judging by what they'd written, I was pretty sure that they'd all just copied that AG's press release and added their own personal commentaries on what a monster I was. The facts were distorted, and their writing was misleading. I didn't see anything that resembled what had actually occurred in the courtroom, what was actually in the written plea agreement or even what was in the accompanying monitor agreement.

And all of it infuriated me—all the articles, the press release, everything. How dare these people who didn't know me—and who hadn't even called me for a comment before writing their articles—spread such lies about me? Or, at the very least, not tell the entire story? I could not find one article that mentioned Detective Kukis' raid of the New Road offices or how he'd treated my people and me as if we were already criminals before the investigation had even begun. Nor did I see one word about the King Solomon's choice that had been laid at my feet: step forward and take the plea or allow the district attorney's office to indict seven people from New Road and potentially ruin my schools. Maybe it hadn't been said in so many words, but Brass did tell my lawyers that while he didn't have enough evidence to convict, he had enough to indict, though he would only do so in order to shake things up and see what fell out. How come there was no mention of any of that?

Because I took the plea, Brass had promised not to print anything that could have hurt the schools, but I didn't see how that promise or any other promise he'd made was being upheld. Instead, there were headlines like "Head of Special-Ed Schools in Parlin Admits Bilking Local Districts of $1.3 Million" and "Head of Private Education Services Corporation Pleads Guilty." NJ.com ran a story titled "Long Branch Woman Admits Bilking Schools," in which it was asserted that I had run an "overbilling scam" for three years and "manipulated" what the state was supposed to reimburse New Road to "illegally boost the profits of the company."

"That's not *true!*" I shouted at my computer, slamming my coffee cup down on the dining room table so hard it spilled. "I didn't overbill anything. There was no scam!" I'd never even taken one cent of the profit that I was legally allowed to according to the state rules. I'd reinvested it all into the schools.

The article went on to throw around words like "fraudulently" and "corrupt" like they didn't mean anything; by the time I was through reading it, I was literally seeing red. I couldn't believe the lack of professionalism, the flagrant abuse of journalistic integrity.

And then I read the user comments at the bottom of the page, and things got a whole lot worse.

"She needs to serve the maximum amount of time," wrote one NJ.com reader. "She is no different than any other criminal!"

"She should not be allowed out of jail until every penny of the restitution is paid," offered another. "Let her rot."

After the first few calls for my lynching, I was ready to turn the computer off and go back to bed—perhaps permanently. As if my day in court hadn't been enough of a blow to my ego, now I knew the public's opinion of me, and it made me feel about two inches tall. All along, I'd believed that I was doing the right thing, the noble thing, but judging by what these people had to say, it didn't matter. They believed whatever the media dished out, and at the moment, I was the entrée.

Scanning over the rest of the comments, I saw more of the same, more readers who thought I was getting everything I deserved. One suggested that I was responsible for the state's rising taxes; one called me a liar outright.

However, surprisingly, some commenters actually supported me.

Wrote one: "Don't believe everything you read. The CEO did not take money from anyone or cost the public a dime… She took the rap herself rather than fight the charges and take the school down with her. The schools actually do a lot of good for children in need of special help."

Said another: "We should keep in mind the one-sidedness of the media and the state. In countless types of these cases, people have been bullied into taking pleas by relentless investigators and prosecutors who themselves would have no issue bending around the rules of the Constitution to see the results they are after."

A third added: "Any business can be shut down based on an inability to financially survive after governmental investigation. It is likely that if she had not taken the plea, the schools would have been shut down, numerous teachers [would have been] out of employment and several students would not have a viable option for their education."

Another: "It is very unfortunate that no one has bothered to mention all the wonderful things that Ellyn Lerner has done for the special needs children who have attended her schools."

And another: "Ellyn Lerner has done incredible things for special education students her entire life… She never took any money for her own gain… The regulations in New Jersey are very strict and learning the whole system is very complex and intricate. Dr. Lerner has paid dearly for this already, being put through over 4 and 1/2 years of investigation…"

And another: "The $1.3 million all went to the students. GO SEE THE SCHOOL. She allowed the students…to be trained in real careers (dental lab assistant, ophthalmology assistant, chef and restaurant management, etc.)... She directed invoices to be broken down into component parts, which resulted in overbilling in one year WITH UNDERBILLING IN YEARS 2-5. Misconduct? Yes. Fraud? ABSOLUTELY NO!!!"

But perhaps this one commenter encapsulated the issue the best: "As taxpayers in the State of NJ we should be up in arms, not about Dr. Lerner and her amazing work and dedication to disabled children, but [about] the AG's office and their inability to let go or acknowledge that a mistake has been made in the name of 'justice.'"

Reading those sentiments, I felt a little bit better—not entirely at ease, but at least they pulled me back from the edge.

Still, I did turn off the laptop and go back to bed for a while. I'd had my fill of news for the day.

Later that afternoon, I sat down once again in front of my computer, cup of coffee in hand. I opened up a Word document and just sat there for a while, staring at the blank, white page on the screen, the wheels in my mind slowly beginning to turn.

"Remorse," I said aloud, then took a sip of my coffee. "Remorse," I repeated, hoping it would start to make some sense to me.

As part of the plea agreement I'd accepted, I was going to be sentenced to some jail time—anywhere from three to five years in a state prison, though under an intensive supervision program (ISP) that could have been reduced to months. Still, I started to panic: Could the attorney general's office have reneged on that promise? Should I really have relied on Bob Brass' word when so much of what he'd promised me had already been scattered by the political winds of his higher-ups? My lawyers' consensus all along was that Brass was basically an honest man who would indeed have honored his word if his bosses hadn't forced him to do what they wanted. I just didn't know whom to trust.

The sentencing hearing was four months away. In the meantime, on the request of my lawyers, I had to write a statement to the court, a letter to the judge, detailing the "crimes" to which I had pled guilty and asking for leniency. The focus of the letter, Rob Kipnees had told me, had to be the remorse that I felt for what I'd allegedly done.

The problem, of course, was that I didn't feel any remorse because I hadn't done anything wrong—not under the law, anyway. Yes, I hadn't followed some state regulations to the letter, but their letters had been vague and open to interpretation, and I just couldn't feel bad about the way I had chosen to view them. Thanks to my directives—which had been, as I've said many times already, approved not only by New Road's external auditors but by our state inspectors as well—my students had access to the best career training and the most state-of-the-art equipment in the state. And, our tuition was eighth-lowest in the state, out of 175 schools in all. Thanks to the way I'd run New Road, our kids enjoyed the highest level of educational resources available at the lowest cost to taxpayers. And I refused to feel remorse for that for even a minute.

In the end, I just couldn't regret committing a crime that didn't exist. I wasn't trying to say that I didn't direct my staff to break down invoices in order to put equipment on the school supply instructional budget rather than the capital budget—I did that indeed. However, the conduct in question should not have been considered a crime. My only legitimate remorse was over the fact that my actions had jeopardized the schools, my people, the students and the districts that placed their students in my trust.

Setting my coffee cup down on the table, I lay my hands across the laptop's keyboard, tapping the keys gently as I thought.

"Remorse," I told myself one more time, focusing my mind on the word. And then I began to type.

Dear Judge Mulvihill:

As Your Honor is aware, I have pleaded guilty to one charge of corporate misconduct in the second degree—an offense for which I accept full responsibility and feel a profound sense of remorse and regret. I write to offer, in my own words, a complete explanation of the circumstances surrounding my offense.

My offense arises out of a directive I gave during my tenure as Chief Executive Officer of New Road Schools. Specifically, I directed the school administrators responsible for purchasing equipment for use in classrooms to break down all large purchases into their component parts. The aim of this directive was to circumvent New Jersey Department of Education regulations, which require all fixed asset expenditures of $2,000 or more to be capitalized and depreciated over five years, rather than charged to current year expenses. As a result of my directive, over $900,000 worth of equipment and new facility startup costs were charged to the 2001-02 budget and the 2002-03 budget, rather than being spread out over the five-year period ending in the 2007-08 school year, as required by the regulations. In addition to that misconduct, I accept responsibility for misallocations involving computers and books that occurred during my tenure as CEO, although I had no knowledge of those misallocations at the time they occurred.

It was illegal and wrong for me to direct my staff to disregard the state regulations in this manner. Looking back, I still cannot believe that I acted with such disregard for the law. I have always tried to live my life in a way that my daughters—and the thousands of students whom I have had the pleasure of working with over the past three decades—could look up to and emulate. I have failed myself, and I have failed them.

Moreover, my actions are totally inconsistent with my decades-long commitment to providing the highest quality education at the lowest possible tuition. I have always worked hard to minimize the cost to the sending districts by keeping tuition rates among the lowest in the state and by declining to seek reimbursements to which the schools and their staff were entitled. For example, from their inception in 1986 through 2004, the New Road schools never billed the sending districts for over *$2.6 million* in reimbursements to which the schools were entitled pursuant to N.J.A.C. 6A:23-4.2(m). By way of brief background on this issue, before the beginning of each school year, the New Jersey Department of Education sets a tentative tuition rate based on the prior year's audited costs. At the end of the school year, the annual audit includes a calculation of the actual cost per student. If the actual cost per student exceeds the tentative rate charged by the private school, the private school is permitted to "back bill" the districts for the true cost of all permissible expenditures made on behalf of or in connection with the program. N.J.A.C. 6A:23-4.2(m). At my direction, the New Road schools did not do so, despite the significant amount of money at stake. My focus was never on seeking the maximum reimbursement from the New Jersey public school districts, but rather on minimizing the costs charged to school districts—while providing the highest level of service to the students of New Jersey.

Another example of my efforts to minimize the cost to the sending districts was my longstanding policy of not considering vehicle expenses as "allowable costs" for the purpose of calculating tuition rates. Although New Jersey Department of Education regulations allow vehicle expenses to be included in the allowable costs charged to the sending districts, N.J.A.C. 6A:23-4.4(a)(18), the New Road schools have never taken advantage of this benefit—despite the fact that I (and some of my staff) traveled extensively between the New Jersey schools.

Likewise, although certainly not an excuse or justification for my actions, I believed at the time I gave the directive at issue here that making the purchases all upfront right before we moved into our new schools would actually save the districts money following years when rent and mortgage costs would have become higher. Nevertheless, I acknowledge that, regrettably, my unlawful actions had the exact opposite effect—at least when viewed from a single-year perspective. Although I knew my actions were unlawful, my intent was never to cause harm to the sending districts, or anyone else for that matter.

Your Honor, no sentence that this court imposes on me could punish me more than I have punished myself. My actions have destroyed my professional and personal reputation, my career, and my self-respect. I am truly sorry for what I have done, and I promise that I will never do anything like this again. I humbly ask Your Honor to consider a sentence that allows me to make amends for my misconduct without removing me from my family or the community I have worked my entire life to serve.

Sincerely,
Ellyn Lerner

When I was done writing, I read it over a few times. It was sufficient; basically, it said what it had to. I emailed it off to Rob Kipnees for approval, and for inclusion in our packet of pre-sentencing information for the judge. Then, I turned off my computer and just tried not to think about it. I'd done what I could. From there on, I would just have to let the chips fall where they may.

Eighteen

After word was out about the plea agreement, a strange phenomenon occurred: People who wanted to support me came out of the woodwork.

It started with a phone call or two at the New Road office, from a psychologist we worked with and, believe it or not, a couple of ex-employees. They'd read about the case in a local newspaper, they'd said, and wanted to see if there was anything they could do to help. Next, I got word that some parents at our schools were coming in and asking the same question. Even a regulatory lawyer with whom we had consulted regarding the Department of Education regulations had called Rob Kipnees to see how he could help on my behalf. I was so taken aback by these unexpected offers that I didn't know exactly what to tell them.

So, as I did with just about every issue in my life at that point, I consulted my lawyer.

"Tell them to call me," Rob told me first, then added, "or tell them to write the judge a letter."

So that was what I did, or what my staff did: Whenever someone called to ask how they could help, we asked them in turn to write a letter of support for me and send it to my lawyer. Over the ensuing months, Rob collected and compiled them, until the date came when he had to submit our sentencing memorandum to the presiding judge.

At the same time, he gave me copies of all the letters he'd received, and to say that I was dumbfounded by the response would be an enormous understatement. When I arrived at his office to pick them up, I was expecting a manila envelope with a few Xeroxed pages in it. Instead, I was handed a heavy, thick, bound book with tabs running down the sides of the pages, marking off the beginning of each letter. There were 129 tabs.

"Rob," I told him. "This is incredible."

He smiled at me. "You have no idea. Those are only the letters I thought were appropriate to include because they didn't talk about how wrong the prosecution was to pursue the case or what an abomination of justice it is. I also kept out the ones that implied that if you did do anything, it wasn't intentional, because we need that intentionality for the plea. I don't want the judge to have any reason to reject it."

I nodded. It made sense. I looked down at the book again, still amazed by the sheer number of letters that had come in. "How many more were there?" I asked, simply out of curiosity.

He looked at me for a moment. "Over a hundred more. Two hundred thirty-five in all."

In the parking lot, I sat in my car with the book on the passenger's seat. As I thumbed through it, my eyes caught a lot of familiar names. There was my husband, of course, and my two daughters. There was my sister-in-law, Elaine, writing on behalf of herself and my brother, Richard. Another sister-in-law, Debbie, and her husband, Neil, had written as well.

Then, there were letters from my oldest and dearest friends—Sandy, Sherry, Ronnie, Enid, Marilyn, Phyllis, Ricki, Lee and Gloria as well as all their husbands. There were letters from newer friends such as Bella and Bruce, Judy and Harvey, Elissa and Sue. My cousins Susan, Eric, Sharon, Barbara, David, Doris, Alice, Mitch, Patrice, Jerry, Dolly and Pat had written, as had my uncle Arthur. There were letters from my neighbors and from friends of friends. From friends of my daughters. Old college buddies—Cynthia, Joanne, Jessica, Corinne. My tax advisor. Rabbi Schapiro from my synagogue. New Road teachers, directors and administrative staff from New Jersey and our other states, both past and present. Colleagues and peers in the education field. The wife of Dave, my former co-CEO. Kathy, my assistant for twenty-three years. And her husband. And her brother. Diane, Jon, Marcelle, Carol, Russ and Doug—all the New Road administration. School directors and principals. Former students. Students' parents. Consultants who had worked with New Road. Our attorneys. Even one of our former auditors took the time to put a word in on my behalf.

The outpouring, the efforts all these people had made for me, was simply overwhelming. I knew that I'd done some great work in my lifetime; I'd had some accomplishments of which I'd been very, very proud. And I'd always tried to influence the people around me positively, from the kids in my schools to the staff in my offices to family to friends to acquaintances.

But never, *never* would I have guessed that I'd affected so many, or that in my time of need, so many would come to aid. Looking at this book, running my palm over its clear-plastic cover, I felt an immense warmth in my heart, and I knew that no matter how things turned out in the end, everything I'd done had been worth it.

Later that evening, I curled up in my favorite living-room chair with the book of letters and set about actually reading them, not just scanning the names.

I began with the letters from my family. In part, my husband wrote to the judge:

> I'd like for you to have the opportunity to know Ellyn as the wife, the mother, the sister, the daughter, the sister-in-law, and so many other roles in which she has expressed her love, devotion and gifts. Through her love, I came to understand the meaning of family and devotion in a way that I never would have been able to experience had I been married to anyone else… She taught me values of forgiveness, letting go of anger, acceptance, tolerance and true love. She has enabled me to become a better person and a better brother, son, and father.

From my younger daughter:

> My mother taught me the value of hard work and
> that if I want something, I have to go after it... She
> further taught me that success is never measured with
> material things and that I need to follow my passion,
> not money. She taught me to always forgive, and most
> of all that I should always take ownership of my own
> failures and mistakes.

From my older daughter:

> In all sincerity, I have never had more admiration and
> respect for anyone than I have developed for my mother
> in these past few years. She has displayed wisdom
> and an amazing ability to love throughout all of this.
> She has admitted her failures and her mistakes while
> protecting the nature of what's good in life, which is,
> among other things, the schools and the foundation
> that she has built to protect the students in her care.

From Bruce Germinsky, a dear friend—he and his wife lived in the
same community as my husband and me, and we spent a lot of time
together both socially and within our religious community:

> My experience with Dr. Lerner has always revealed,
> actually taught me, people first, business second, for
> without the people, without the students, there is no
> business. For the past 20-some years, Dr. Lerner has
> worked tirelessly, not for her schools' balance sheet or
> profit and loss statements, not for her own personal
> wealth, but for the development and well-being of
> literally thousands of very, very special children and
> young adults. Dr. Lerner has taught me, in many
> ways, to focus on the good in people, even in times
> of extreme personal distress... Dr. Lerner has always

enriched my life from a professional, personal and spiritual perspective.

From Judith Goldman, another good friend—she was a former elementary school teacher who had recently bought a tennis club when we'd met:

> I met Ellyn Lerner six years ago. I immediately recognized a kindred spirit in that we were both dedicated to our families and to our businesses. I thought that I was serious and passionate about building a business of which I could be proud, until I met Ellyn, visited her schools, and realized what dedication and passion really are. She lived and breathed for those schools and for those children. I admired (even to the point of awe) how she spent every day thinking of ways to reach those special ed children and improve their lives through her schools. She urged me to visit her schools so that, as a friend and fellow educator, I could understand her passion. I can only say that I was overwhelmingly blown away by what I saw! I have never seen any educational institution that comes close to Ellyn's New Jersey schools.
>
> I respect Ellyn more than any friend I have ever had. Her passion for education and her idealism are inspirational. I feel honored to call her my friend…
>
> She represents the best of mothers, friends, teachers, and decent human beings.

From Keith White, director of a High Road school in Maryland:

> I have had the privilege and honor to serve with and learn from Ms. Lerner since December of 1999. Under her tutelage and leadership I have grown both professionally as well as personally… Through her perseverance and dedication to her staff's growth, my

colleagues and I have professionally blossomed, providing our schools with a higher quality of service...

Personally, my relationship with Ms. Lerner has been invaluable. She has helped me to identify and address the challenges that blocked my growth, as well as build upon my strengths as a leader. I have been able to take the lessons I've learned from her and pass them on to my staff, aiding them in their professional development. And most importantly, she has inspired me to become a better person. I honestly do not know where I would be today were it not for the mentoring and leadership of Ms. Lerner and the positive culture of the company she founded.

From Annette Hockenjos, my replacement as executive director of New Road, since I had to give up the position upon accepting the plea agreement—she had worked for New Road for twenty-four years already at that point:

I have met many special people in my lifetime, and all of them have a special place in my life and in my heart. But every so often, there steps forward an individual who is so extraordinary, who so imprints herself on our minds and hearts, that her mark is indelible, invaluable, and irreplaceable—a person to honor and cherish for as long as we live. For me, that person is Ellyn Lerner... [Her] leadership and vision has singlehandedly shaped my professional life and given a clear and direct purpose to all of my days for close to a quarter of a century.

From Michael Kaufman, president and CEO of Specialized Education Services, Inc., a former sister company of the New Road Schools that also had to be divested as a result of the press surrounding my involvement in this case (there are more than thirty High Road and Sierra

Schools located in Maryland, Connecticut, California, Delaware, Rhode Island, Illinois and the District of Columbia):

> Time after time, people have told me how they've been touched by Ellyn in positive, profound ways. Her heart is both generous and resilient; her mind is both powerful and receptive; and her devotion to those she cares for is both fierce and tender. As a mother, wife, friend, and business partner, she loves deeply and is loved deeply. She is a singular individual who has made her own way in this world brilliantly. When it comes to the kind of person she is, Ellyn Lerner is remarkable...
>
> Ellyn has an uncanny ability to see the light inside of someone—who they want to be, what they want to become—and then she applies her ample skills and know-how toward leading that person to their truest and best self. I know she did this for me, and the man I am today is deeply indebted to her for that. Never will you find a stronger advocate, a more dedicated coach in your corner... To me, she is the very personification of the word "leader." Indicative of her great respect for her colleagues, she has never asked me to do anything I'd be uncomfortable doing, and she has always extended great effort on promoting the personal and professional growth of her staff...
>
> Obviously, I am a huge fan of Ellyn Lerner. I could go on and on listing her admirable attributes, but the point I want to make is that I think so highly of her not because she hired me and trained me, not because she built a successful business from the ground up, but because she's earned each and every positive thing I have to say about her.

From Ellen Gaske, executive director of one of High Road's schools in Maryland:

> Over the past years, Ellyn has been my most trusted mentor and the one and only person I would seek out for advice for my school. I have complete confidence in her skills and trust her without question. I could never imagine our company without her at the helm.

From Vicki Grant, a New Road educator since 1985:

> Ellyn has taught me numerous things about being a teacher and running a classroom. She has spent many hours coaching me in my classroom and helping me every step of the way. All of the college courses I took could not have taught me the amount of information and hands-on experiences that Ellyn has given me over the years...
>
> I feel as though Ellyn has given me wings. She allowed me to become the teacher that I am today. She is an outstanding woman who is intelligent and caring. I am forever indebted to her, both professionally and personally.

From Greg Marancik, a brilliant, young High Road School director for the past six years:

> ...I have been blessed with the opportunity to live out a career dream in an organization that [Ellyn] has created, grow both personally and professionally under her leadership and get to know an amazing woman for whom I could not have any more respect...to [an] extent which I will never successfully be able to convey in this letter, [Ellyn] has greatly touched and impacted my life, for which I will forever be thankful.
>
> Through Ellyn and the schools she has created, I

have found a place that shares my passion for these very special students… Because of Ellyn, I have found a place that has allowed me to grow as a person, educator, and leader and to find a special meaning in my life that I would most likely never have found anywhere else.

From Diane O'Donnell, the program director at New Road School of Ocean County, New Jersey—she was a founding member of the New Road staff, joining us as a teacher in 1986:

Ellyn Lerner saw potential in me and encouraged me to pursue a leadership role within the organization. Ellyn guided me to see myself in a different perspective, one that I don't think I would have discovered on my own. Ellyn believed in me in a manner that empowered me to challenge myself to a level that I was unaware I possessed. For this, I will always be grateful to Ellyn for her unique ability to see goodness and potential in people.

From Carrie Spies, the longest-tenured staff member in the High Road schools in Maryland and currently a regional director:

I have been forever changed by this company in every good way a person can be changed…

I have seen hundreds of students come through our doors frustrated and hating the educational system who now love school and smile all the time because they have experienced firsthand the satisfaction of learning and of making positive contributions to society. We can all thank Ellyn Lerner for that gift.

…Ellyn brought to the workplace innovative concepts like compassion and strength, leading with empathy and accountability, and always using authenticity with affinity with others… The staff who work for this company stay at this company because they feel valued and know they will rise and be promoted based on their skill and desire, not on politics and favoritism.

From Howard Margolis, professor emeritus of reading disabilities and special education, Queens College of CUNY, who had completed an expert-opinion report on New Road's schools during the investigation:

> ...she has done so much good for untold numbers of children with disabilities and can still do so much to make the lives of children with disabilities so much better. Simply put, her knowledge of special education, her ability to motivate teachers and staff, and her dedication to children is critical to the lives of so many children with disabilities.

From Danielle Peck, program director and director of education for High Road in Baltimore:

> Ellyn has had only a positive impact on my life. I am a better person, wife, mother, administrator and teacher for knowing her... She helped me see that students should not be "warehoused" but given every opportunity to be the most productive citizen in their community. Ellyn promotes opportunities for our students that I can say other programs and schools do not. She believes the more students we impact, the more families we impact, the more communities we impact, and the better place this world will be. That is a very big undertaking and I am proud to be part of it.

From Harvey Goldman, a friend and an accounting consultant and expert whom my lawyers had hired to work on the New Road case:

> ...during the period in which I have been privileged to know Dr. Lerner, I have always admired her dedication to her students, her desire to provide them with an exceptional educational experience, and her desire to be an innovator in developing curriculum to help her special ed students achieve results beyond normal expectations.
>
> ...I would urge the court to demonstrate leniency in sentencing Dr. Lerner, recognizing that there was no fraudulent intent in the matter, that there was no personal benefit received, and that all of the expenditures in question were legitimate and solely directed at improving the quality of the educational experience received by her students. I can further assure you that as a result of her misconduct and directive to break down large scale purchases into component parts, there has been no personal gain, no gain to the company over time, and no financial loss to the school districts when viewed from a multi-year perspective.

In the back of the book, Rob Kipnees had stuck in a few loose sheets. Taking them out, I saw that they were photocopies of a letter written by my father, just four days before his death on July 11, 2008. He had dictated it to my brother, Richard. My dad had been an IRS agent for over thirty years, specializing in the auditing of corporations with foreign subsidiaries. After he retired from there at age fifty-five, he worked for a private company as a tax specialist for another decade. He had a bachelor's degree in business and a CPA license; he'd even graded CPA exams for a while. Before I'd hired Mark as New Road's CFO, I had relied on Dad for financial advice for my company. He'd even reviewed New Road's audits from 1986 through 1996.

The point is, when it came to financial stuff, my dad knew what he was talking about, and anything he'd had to say about my case undoubtedly would have been dead on.

Unfortunately, his letter also did a lot of railing against the system that Rob Kipnees was afraid might put a bad taste in the judge's mouth. So, Dad's letter was excluded from the official packet. I was disappointed, but I understood. And I was thankful that Rob had thought to put a copy of it into the book just for me.

In part, my father's letter read:

> First, Judge, I would like to say as a former IRS agent, that everyone knows that expensing vs. capitalizing is the grayest area of tax law and I would assume of the New Jersey law that my daughter has broken. My daughter has so much integrity, that once when I asked her to put me on the payroll of the school because I gave a lot of advisory time and reviewing time, she refused and told me that this business was a taxpayer supported business (local taxes subsidized the tuition reimbursement) and didn't think it would be right to #1 put a family member on the payroll and #2 have to use tax money to support my time.
>
> During my free consultations, I was the one that told her to break down the invoices into smaller components so as to expense the expenditures in one year rather than carrying them as assets on the balance sheet. I talked to her auditors at the time (about 1990) and although I forget their names I remember that they agreed with my suggestion. Ellyn, my daughter, specifically asked me if that was allowed and I told her ABSOLUTELY YES. I explained that the government would actually look favorably at this because it would not make a difference tax-wise, and because of her special regulations, it would actually deflate the total value of the company because she would not be carrying assets on the balance sheet if she expensed. (In other words, if she capitalized everything as an asset, the value of the company would go up because of the book value of the assets.) And anything that deflates your own personal gain, the government would like.
>
> ...the guilt that I feel for having given my daughter

advice that would have ended her up in a situation like this is the worst guilt I have ever felt.

I paused there; I wasn't sure if I wanted to read any more. Dad had been eighty-eight at the time of his death, but in decent health. He'd passed suddenly in the night, while trying to get up out of his bed to use the bathroom. He'd collapsed. There had been no autopsy but we all believed it had been a heart attack…and I believed that this guilt he felt had contributed to that. Guilt over my case, over what I was going through. I still have a hard time reconciling myself with that.

Drying my eyes, I went on reading:

> My daughter is a wonderful child who visits me every single day (except if she travels) and does my medications for the month. Her visits sustain my life since my wife died almost eight years ago.
>
> Your honor, I spoke to Ellyn's lawyers two years ago and told them all this information. I actually yelled at her for spending so much on legal fees and that this would never amount to a criminal charge… If you knew her, you would know that she has more honesty and integrity than anyone. When she went over her budget (you know there is a way to submit reimbursement for additional expenses from the government), I told her to go after the reimbursement—but she refused. She said that any school needs discipline in managing their money even if it's state money and she didn't want to get in the habit of going over budget. So she chose to eat the loss (something I would never advise). Over the ten-year period that I advised her (1986-1996), she left $2.6 million on the table. I had no idea it came to that much.
>
> So, Judge, please call it a wash and don't make my daughter suffer any more than she has already over these past four years since I went into assisted living and the criminal case began. I read the press coverage of this plea deal and I felt so badly for my wonderful daughter who has given love, respect, and honor

to me, her family, and the government of New Jersey. Have a little "rachmunus" (it's a Jewish word meaning compassion) on my daughter and her family.

———

After a while, I had to close the book and set it aside—not because I was tired, but because the embarrassment was too much for me. I did not want to read these letters—and I do not reprint them here—just to hear how much people loved me or how great I was. In fact, all the praise seemed sort of morbid to me, kind of like hearing my own eulogy. I simply felt that because so many people had gone to such trouble for me, I had to repay the favor and read all they had done. It was the least I could do. My simple thanks surely never would have been enough.

Besides, these letters would be submitted to the judge who would decide my sentence, the person with the power to perhaps keep me out of prison. When I walked into that courtroom on October 3, I had to know what kind of ammunition I was carrying.

Nineteen

After all the drama I had been through—the years of the investigation, taking the plea agreement, the months of legal back and forth, the bad press—showing up for the sentencing hearing was almost anticlimactic.

I was eager to hear what would become of me, but of course I feared the worst, even though my lawyers had prepared me well ahead of time. I knew exactly what *could* happen: The judge could sentence me to three, four or five years in prison; if I was accepted into the intensive supervision program the actual incarceration time could then be dropped down to three, five or six months, respectively. I had resigned myself to the fact that there would be jail time. That was a given considering the plea agreement and the prosecutor's clause that there would be an appeal if I had been given a probationary sentence. Mostly I was terrified that the judge would deny the ISP altogether even though the State had set forth no opposition to it in the plea agreement. What can I say—after four and a half years of broken promises and arbitrary, capricious enforcement of regulations, I wasn't feeling too trusting of the officers of the court or the justice system.

I arrived at the courthouse first thing in the morning on October 3, 2008, with my husband and daughters by my side as well as Rob Kipnees and Melissa Lozner, another one of my attorneys from the same firm. Joe Hayden, New Road's attorney, was already there, as was Bob Brass. In the back of the courtroom, the gallery was full, with more people waiting outside who couldn't get seats. So many of my family, friends, colleagues and staff from the schools had shown up to support me that it was standing room only. I almost couldn't believe it.

"It's a mob scene," Rob muttered to me as we made our way through the crowd. Hands reached out to touch me, to squeeze my arm or pat my shoulder reassuringly. I smiled, said hello to whomever I could, and tried not to break out in tears.

"I know, it's great, isn't it?" I replied as we found our seats at the front of the courtroom. I looked back at the gallery again, in shock at the sheer number of people there.

"I don't know," Rob said. "I mean, it's a great show of support for you. I just hope it doesn't piss off the judge."

I hadn't thought about that, and now that I did, it made me nervous all over again. I turned around and faced the front of the room, folded my hands in my lap and just waited for the judge to arrive.

After a few agonizing minutes, he did, and I was relieved to see that he didn't look annoyed by the semi-chaos brewing in the back of the room. In fact, he seemed merely surprised by it. I didn't know quite what to expect from this judge—he was new, and I didn't know much about him. Judge Mulvihill, the one for whom we had prepared the pre-sentencing report and to whom all my supporters had written letters, had mysteriously recused himself just two days earlier. Though we'd never found out exactly why, my lawyers and I had come up with two possibilities: he knew someone who worked at New Road or attended one of our schools, or he did not feel that he could, in good conscience, sentence me to incarceration for my so-called crimes. If he didn't send me to jail, though, he would not uphold my plea agreement. He was bound by the law. Perhaps, I thought, he was also bound by his morals, and thus he recused himself.

Whatever the reason, I was upset about the turn of events. Judge Mulvihill had seemed sympathetic toward me, as much as he could be under the law, and I believed that he was going to give me a fair shake. This new guy, Judge Ferencz, also had a good reputation, but I didn't have the same history with him. Who knew what he would do? I took a deep breath. I would just have to wait and see.

Judge Ferencz stood behind his bench for a moment, surveying all of us, then leaned over to his bailiff and whispered something. I peered at Rob Kipnees, who simply looked back at me and shrugged.

"Ladies and gentlemen," the judge announced then, "due to the unexpectedly large turnout today, we're going to move to a bigger courtroom so that everyone will have a seat. Please bear with us while we find out which one is empty—and large enough for all of us."

I sat back and looked over at Rob again, and this time we were both smiling. I couldn't have asked for a better start.

≈

A half hour or so later, we were all—the judge, the bailiff, me, the attorneys and all my supporters—settled into the largest courtroom in the complex, and finally, we were ready to get the hearing underway. Wasting no time, the judge took the bench and banged his gavel.

"Counsel," he began, "I've reviewed the presentencing report, along with what could only be called an extraordinary outpouring of concern and care from the citizens with whom Ms. Lerner has worked and come in contact."

This seemed like a good sign to me—that he wasn't bothered by the overwhelming show of support from all sides. Glancing back at the audience, at the office and school staff, at my husband and daughters, my friends and neighbors, I said a silent "thank you" for all their care and concern, for all the trouble they'd gone to for me. And I was just so glad that in the end, it was counting for something.

The judge then asked the attorneys if there were any additions or deletions to or inaccuracies in the presentencing report. Rob Kipnees objected to how the report characterized my "crimes" as being motivated by greed, and he, the judge and Brass debated that for a while. Sitting behind the defendant's table, I fidgeted in my seat and tried to listen to them, but concentration just wasn't coming to me. I wondered if this was what the entire hearing was going to be like.

"The violation to which Ellyn Lerner pled guilty," Rob was saying as I half listened, "involved her directions relating to the purchasing and itemizing of equipment and supplies to render each component under two thousand dollars, the New Jersey statutory threshold delineating a capital item. The avoidance of this threshold, by breaking down a large-scale purchase into its individual components, was the factual basis for the criminal offense of corporate misconduct. The result of this misconduct had the effect of overstating tuition the year that the equipment was purchased. However, it also had the effect of under-stating tuition in the following four years. Over a five-year period, the net effect of the two accounting treatments—expensing or capitaliz-ing—was zero. It was just a matter of timing."

"A matter of timing," Judge Ferencz repeated softly, as if talking to himself as he flipped through the pages of the presentencing report. Then, he looked back up at us. "Is there anything else, Counsel?"

"Yes, Your Honor," Rob replied. "With the Court's permission, I would ask if Your Honor would first consider hearing from one individual on behalf of all who are present—Dr. Michael Kaufman, CEO of Specialized Education Services, Inc., the former sister schools of New Road."

The judge glanced at the audience, where Mike was getting up from his seat. "I would. Why don't you come on up over here, sir? State who you are with some clarity, so the record is clear."

Making his way to a podium near the counsels' tables, Mike looked serious, some typewritten notes clutched in his hand. "My name is Michael Kaufman," he said into the podium's microphone, leaning over a bit to speak directly into it.

"Okay," replied the judge, then motioned for Mike to continue.

"Thank you very much," Mike said. "Your Honor, I speak as the joint voice of the myriad managers, staff members, parents and students that comprise the New Road and High Road families—nearly one hundred of whom are present here today. It is my belief that this country owes a large debt to Ellyn Lerner for the immense contribution she has made to the field of special education and the multitude of advancements she has facilitated for the special needs children who inhabit it. I've been watching that contribution up close and personal for over a decade now, and I can tell you beyond a shadow of a doubt that the woman you see before you is a truly remarkable individual. She is a loving wife, a dedicated mother and a fiercely loyal friend. She is natural-born leader, an inspiring trailblazer, an effective activist and advocate."

I looked down at my lap, folding and unfolding my fingers. All this praise again—well deserved, I imagined, but it never failed to make me feel just a little bit uncomfortable.

"And like many remarkable people," Mike continued, "Ellyn Lerner has been blessed with a host of gifts that she unceasingly bestows upon others. She has been gifted with the *vision* to formulate and found an education company that has led thousands of challenged students down the high road to academic success via the innovative programs and targeted interventions she created. She has been gifted with uncommon *compassion* and *strength,* the first of which fuels her heart to want to make the world a more fulfilling and productive place for as many people as possible, the second of which gives her the fortitude and perseverance to effect the changes she envisions."

I nodded, thinking about the thousands of students, the hundreds of employees and just all the people I'd known in my lifetime upon which I'd been able to have some positive impact along the way. Of this, I was not embarrassed; helping people to better themselves had been the whole point of my life. It was good to hear a reminder that not only had I accomplished it, but that people had noticed.

At the podium, Michael went on. "She has been equally gifted with a generous soul, a pioneering spirit and a brilliant mind. But of all her gifts, I've been most impressed by her uncanny ability to shine a light on the hidden talents and abilities deep within others and bring them to the fore for the betterment of all. My colleagues and I could all tell you a similar story of how Ellyn coached us to become the devoted educators we are today; how she taught us invaluable lessons about self-accountability, self-reliance, self-honesty, how she acted as the most vocal and visible champion we ever had in our corner before or are likely to have in our corner again. I would not be the man I am today—the proud leader of this company, the heir to her legacy, the committed friend and the most loving father I can be—if I didn't have Ellyn's beacon beckoning me ever onward, her lighthouse offering guidance and solace when the inevitable storms hit."

I bowed my head again and reached a hand up quickly to wipe away my tears. Words cannot express how incredibly bittersweet Michael's speech was to me, same as all those letters people had written for me and all the kind words of support I'd heard up until that point. I had always wanted to help people, but to hear just how profound and far-reaching my impact had been…it was the most touching, beautiful, inspiring and, given the situation, saddest thing I had ever heard. And I just couldn't hold back the emotions it aroused in me.

"To my mind, Ellyn Lerner is an incredibly gifted woman," Michael continued. "And sometimes incredibly gifted people slip up… Sometimes they're so focused on the big picture—the life-altering measures and the life-changing results—that they use poor judgment or flawed methods in their rush to accomplish truly noble and valiant goals.

"Your Honor, I am in no way trying to make light of the transgressions that led us to this courtroom today. But I am trying to put them in perspective, because the big picture does matter in life, because it *has* to matter in life, doesn't it? And it is from that perspective that I and my colleagues entreat you, from the bottoms of our hearts, to show as much mercy and be as lenient as possible when sentencing Dr. Lerner today. All of us who know her well know her to be a woman of unshakable principles, unquestionable character and undaunted integrity. That's who she is; that's her bottom line. And yet we're here today because this utterly *extraordinary* woman did a very *ordinary* thing by making a mistake in her professional life—a mistake that had nothing whatsoever to do with personal gain and everything to do with a one-time, uncharacteristic lapse in judgment. She has already paid dearly for this mistake; she has taken full responsibility for her missteps and is courageously prepared now to face whatever sentence Your Honor may deem appropriate. I can only hope that my words—that our joint admiration for this woman, our united and merited support for her—might help to minimize the price still yet to be paid."

That was my hope as well. Looking at Judge Ferencz, who had his eyes and his concentration firmly on Michael, I silently prayed that he was really listening, and that he would take to heart the words that my friend was offering.

"The final legal judgment, of course, falls to you, Your Honor," Michael concluded. "But I hope the collective judgment of special educators, students and parents will weigh heavily on your decision concerning this woman, since Ellyn Lerner is someone who puts others' needs in front of her own, someone who makes others' dreams her own dreams, someone who believes in others more than they believe in themselves. I'm very grateful that you've given me—given all of us—this chance to champion our champion, to fight on her behalf, as she's always done for us, and I thank you very much for your time and consideration."

When he was through, he simply returned to his seat in the audience; turning to give him a grateful smile, I noted that there was not a dry eye in the house—with the exception of the judge, of course, and good old Bob Brass, who sat at his table, staring straight ahead, no sign of any sort of emotion whatsoever on his face.

"Before you begin, Counsel," the judge said then, breaking into the silence, "let me tell you that I've reviewed what—for the record, I've already described, but let me say again—is just an extraordinary outpouring of letters. It's beyond sympathy. They show that there is a community of people that thinks exceptionally highly of this defendant and consider her to be, as your one speaker indicated, an exceptional woman."

Again, this was a good sign. Obviously all the support that had come in for me had done the job we'd hoped it would. He'd already mentioned it twice.

"Having said that," he went on, "I ask you to be mindful in your presentation that this Court is not so much concerned with sympathy as it is with the law and the aggravating and mitigating factors as they exist."

And that made me feel a little less warm and fuzzy. Of course, the judge had to be impartial; he had to abide by the law. But to hear that he had to ignore the obvious sympathy he felt for me and my situation… well, it just didn't give me a whole lot of hope for the final outcome.

Regardless of my feelings, the proceedings continued. The judge called on Rob Kipnees to present his case first, and Rob delivered another glowing soliloquy on my behalf, citing my personal and professional accomplishments, how much my staff admired me and how great my schools were. He then railed against the claim in the presentencing report that I had committed these so-called crimes for my own profit, noting that I had always funneled every penny back into the schools instead of taking anything for myself. He talked about how I had forgone backbilling the state—an acceptable, *allowable* practice—to the tune of $2.6 million, a loss that I had chosen to let my organization absorb rather than burden the school districts. He noted how all the expenses in question would have been allowable if they had been capitalized over a five-year period.

He acknowledged that I took responsibility for everything and abided by every aspect of the agreement I had made with the state, including a $914,000 restitution that involved crediting each affected school district with reclassified expenditures from New Road's expense budget and rebilling the same district for the same amount of money as the capital asset items (which would be paid for over a five-year period). I had also divested myself of both employment in and ownership of the New Road schools.

Along the way, Rob managed to get in a few jabs at Brass, calling his plea agreement "draconian" and scoffing at the DAG's assertion that only jail time—and not all the humiliating, gut-wrenching trauma I had already gone through over the last four and a half years—would deter me (and others like me) from committing further crimes. Just the opposite, Rob asked the judge to be as lenient as possible and sentence me only to three years with ISP, the lowest amount of time allowable by law.

"Mr. Brass," Judge Ferencz said when Rob was done. "I am fully aware that I must, under the law, incarcerate Ms. Lerner on the basis of the plea agreement that the attorney general's office struck with her. But I don't suppose you're willing to rethink your negotiated plea?"

For a moment, I felt a glimmer of hope—just a tiny, slight ray of possibility. Brass had the power to call the whole thing off, or at least to rescind the request for incarceration. To paraphrase one of America's legal giants, US Attorney General Robert H. Jackson, in his famous speech to federal prosecutors in 1940, a prosecutor has the power to control other people's lives—and especially their liberty. A prosecutor represents a powerful force, whether he chooses to be charitable or malicious. A good prosecutor, one who is concerned with the well-being of his nation's citizens, will possess an even mixture of passion for the law and compassion for his fellow man. He will be on the side of justice, not vengeance, and he should be more concerned with doing what is fair rather than with getting a conviction.

I'd read Jackson's speech while doing my legal research, and it had given me new insight into how Bob Brass worked—and maybe even a little bit of respect for him. He was a soldier for the attorney general's office, and that was a tough job. In muscling a plea from me, as it seemed to me his superiors had wanted him to do, he had performed his job effectively. And now, I knew, he wasn't going to budge. He'd worked too hard on it. The attorney general's office, I thought, wanted this conviction not for fairness, not for justice, but for headlines and political gain. And they weren't going to let me off the hook.

"No, Your Honor," he said, and I closed my eyes, wondering why I had bothered to get my hopes up even for a brief moment.

While I sat there in darkness for a minute, trying to center my thoughts, Brass went on to say that the state would not enter an opinion on how many years my sentence should be or whether or not I got into the intensive supervision program. I tried not to hear the smugness in his voice, the confident way he spoke about me as if I were the most despicable soon-to-be convict he'd ever had the pleasure of ruining.

When I opened my eyes again, he was trying to convince the judge that on the contrary to Rob Kipnees' previous statement, I had in fact made a profit from my actions. Brass' argument?

"The assets and the profit increased the net worth of the schools, of which she's a fifty-percent shareholder."

Now, the irony of this argument was that because I had expensed all the items in question rather than recording them as assets, the balance sheet actually showed fewer assets and therefore actually decreased the book value of the school. Profit, he said? Well, where was it? Where was that 2.5 percent that I was allowed? It was nowhere, because it didn't exist. I didn't take it! Absolutely no one got any profit out of this deal.

And the judge seemed to catch on to that as well. "So it's the State's position," he said with what I thought was a bit of an incredulous look on his face, "that she was building an empire on the back of illegal reporting?"

Brass stuck his chin up in the air, haughty and proud of his ill-conceived—and, frankly, just ridiculous—accusation. "That's correct."

He then launched into some convoluted explanation about how I'd also received profits from sending equipment bought in New Jersey to some of our schools in Connecticut, referring to all the stuff that had been shipped there completely without my knowledge, as I had stated at my allocution. By Brass' reasoning, because we received a set amount for expenses for each student in Connecticut and this equipment reduced the actual money we had to spend on each student, our profits were increased. In theory, in a general way, it made sense. But specifically applied to my situation, it simply wasn't true. The amount of money that we spent on each student in Connecticut, in terms of books and computers, was higher than the amount we spent per pupil in New Jersey. If he'd looked into it just a slight amount, he would have found that. This theory of his was far-fetched and completely without proof.

"Do you have," the judge asked Brass, "any indication that she took a profit from those schools? Did you see any profit coming back to her?

Any checks being deposited in her account? I know that you had all of her financial information subpoenaed. Did you find anything coming back to this defendant?"

Brass cleared his throat. I noticed his cheeks beginning to glow, as if he were having a sudden hot flash, a wave of discomfort. "The only indication we have," he admitted, "is that when the schools in Connecticut billed the state or the individual school districts there, they entered into an agreement based upon bidding for the school contracts. And she was able to underbid them. So she profited either by increasing the enrollment in her Connecticut schools or by building more programs."

I shook my head. This was ludicrous and absolutely erroneous. I turned towards the back and exchanged a look of incredulous confusion with Karin, the Connecticut regional manager. Connecticut had no bidding process, so how could I have underbid anything? They simply set a rate and we followed their guidance. Besides, none of this had been in the plea agreement, and to bring it up now was simply wrong. Brass couldn't prove that I had made any profit in any real way, so he was fishing for connections that were tenuous at best—this one, in fact, was downright fabricated. I wondered why the judge was even entertaining it.

However, what he said next made me believe that he wasn't. "As Counsel represented, the twelve point five percent profit that she could have taken on this one million dollars' worth of equipment and supplies that had been expensed rather than capitalized would have only amounted to twelve thousand five hundred dollars, which she never took but reinvested in the schools. Do you disagree with this? Or, again, do you have any proof that she took any money personally?"

Again, Brass cleared his throat. "We don't see a flow of money," he finally admitted, and I could have jumped out of my chair and let out a cry of victory—if I hadn't been crying so hard, and so riveted to my chair.

Finally moving on from that subject, Brass went into the same factors that Kipnees had addressed, including the restitution I'd already paid and whether or not throwing me in jail would serve as a deterrent to other would-be criminals. Brass, of course, believed that it would. He also posited that my actions could not be attributed to a "lapse of judgment" because I had entered a guilty plea, which meant, it seemed, that I had done everything on purpose, and with ill intent.

When he was done, Judge Ferencz told me it was my turn to make a statement if I wished to, and I did. I'd spent the few days leading up to the hearing writing out just what I wanted to say, then going over it with my lawyers and narrowing it down considerably. Since I'd never had a trial, this was my one chance to tell my side of the story, but at the same time, I had to do the old remorse song and dance so that the judge might take pity on me and sentence me leniently. With my hands thus tied, I thought I'd come up with a fair statement, one that got out what I wanted to express while still managing to bend to what the Court would want to hear.

As I tried to stand up from my chair, the room was completely silent. Tears ran down my face and dripped onto the paper containing my statement.

"Take your time," the judge told me gently. "If you'd like to sit, that would be fine."

I nodded at him and smiled, then sat back down. "I apologize, Your Honor. I can't help getting emotional about this."

After taking a moment to compose myself, I was ready to begin. "Aside from watching my children grow up, building these schools for students with disabilities has been the pride and joy of my life. My life has been enriched in ways that I could never put into words. Watching a child read a book for the first time in his life, witnessing families actually loving their time together with the child that was previously impulsive, inattentive, and a significant behavior problem, and seeing students come back to visit us as young adults with long-term employment and families of their own, that's—that has created immeasurable elation during my entire career.

"My mistakes and my lapses of judgment—" I looked pointedly over at Bob Brass. "Yes, *judgment*, could have jeopardized the whole organization in which I so believe and to which I have given my all. I could have hurt countless numbers of teachers, school directors and principals who believed in me and trusted me, many of whom are in this room today, not to mention the children, their families and the public school systems that placed faith in my ability to serve their students well.

"I feel that I must put this apology into writing for all those that were affected by my lapse in judgment. The misconduct to which I do admit and I plead guilty was as a result of a directive that I gave to principals and directors when making large-scale purchases. My directive knowingly circumvented a Department of Education regulation that required the capitalization of fixed assets over two thousand dollars.

"Though this is not a defense for my actions, Your Honor, I really did believe at the time that by expensing the purchases all upfront, right before we moved into two new schools, we would be saving the districts money in the following years when the rent and the mortgage costs would have become higher. I also thought that I would save the districts the finance charges that would have been incurred had I billed the purchases over a five-year period. But what I did was inexcusable. I took the regulations into my own hands, used my own logic and gave the direction to structure the invoices under two thousand dollars so that these purchases would be paid for at a time when we thought we could afford them as opposed to over the next few years, when money would be scarcer.

"In retrospect, it was, indeed, a lapse of judgment that made me give that directive. No matter how good the intention was, the behavior indicated that I disregarded the very regulations that gave us fiscal integrity and the discipline needed to run an efficient and effective organization. Moreover, I put one hundred and seventy-five employees in jeopardy and three hundred seventy-five students who need, value and deserve the services that New Road Schools provide. I also put at risk the trust of the various school districts that I believe deserved better. They deserved faithful and unwavering execution of all the regulations.

"Once again, Your Honor, I offer my sincerest apologies to the Court and to all those whose lives have been affected by the investigation and by my misconduct. I am certain I will never do anything of this nature again in my life. I ask forgiveness of all of the employees who have come here today, of all those school districts who have entrusted their students to the organization that I love. And I pray that I can be given another chance one day to demonstrate my commitment to the education of New Jersey students with special needs. I have gained a lot of insight and perspective. And, Your Honor, I have gained the courage to stand up and do what is right in this case. I will continue to do everything that I can to redress the damage that was caused as a result of my misconduct."

And that was it. When I was done, there was simply silence. This was unlike any other speech I had ever made—there was no applause, no cheering, no acknowledgment whatsoever of what I had said. I hadn't expected anything, really; this was a courtroom, after all. But the quiet in there at that moment was oppressive. I almost felt like I should stand up and apologize again just to feel some sort of closure.

"What an unfortunate and extraordinarily awful position you find yourself in," Judge Ferencz said, breaking the stillness, and the kindness in his voice almost knocked the wind out of me. "There is very little question in my mind that your motivation was not out of personal financial greed. I don't see it in the well over a hundred letters that were sent to me. I don't see it in the expressions of the people who have come to support you."

He looked back over my head, at the audience behind me, and for a moment I turned and did the same. I was greeted by a sea of the most hopeful faces I had ever seen in my life. Everyone was on the edge of their seats, hanging on the judge's every word.

"As I review the facts of the case," he went on, still scanning them as he spoke, "it saddens the Court to find itself in the position of having to sentence someone with the history and commitment that you have." He paused, then turned back to his presentencing report. "As I look at the State's argument for aggravating factors, they do exist. There is, given the nature of what you did for a living, given your interaction with the State, your obligations to three hundred seventy students, a clear need—almost an unfortunate, overwhelming need—to state with clarity that the conduct that you participated in cannot be tolerated. I believe you're not going to do this again. But it doesn't involve just you."

And with that, he went over, one by one, the aggravating and mitigating factors in the presentencing report, finding, in the end, that the latter heavily outweighed the former. However, as he had said at the top of the hearing, the Court would not be swayed by sympathy. Everything about his demeanor and the words he said showed me that he really did feel for my situation and that he understood why I'd done what I'd done. Still, he was bound by the law and by my plea agreement. He could not deviate from either; he had to incarcerate me. If he didn't the State would appeal, and it would all end up the same anyway.

So, the judge did what he ultimately had to do. "It is the Court's sentence," he announced, "that you be committed to the care and custody of the Commission of Corrections for the minimum term of three years. That is the least this Court feels it can impose legally. For while there is a five-year exposure, this Court does not feel that sentence is appropriate given the overwhelming mitigating factors. But given the existence and strength of the plea agreement, incarceration is warranted and is so imposed. I'm also going to place in the sentencing of this defendant that this Court does not oppose application to and acceptance into the ISP program. That is out of this Court's hands, ma'am, but I'm letting them know that I'm not opposing it."

That, at least, was a relief, and I let out a big breath and sat back in my seat. The worst of it, I thought, was over. I would be allowed into the ISP; my jail time would be minimal. After everything else I had gone through, this seemed like a blessing. A small one, because the biggest damage had already been done. I'd already lost almost everything. But still, I was thankful. I had to be.

"Lastly," Judge Ferencz went on, "Mr. Kipnees has requested that you be permitted to surrender on Monday. Mr. Brass, on the other hand, has asked that you be treated as any other nonviolent offender who comes before this Court and remanded immediately. It's a reasonable request. But this isn't about every other defendant, Mr. Brass. And each defendant in this court shall be treated as an individual and have the law applied to him or her as best this court can, fairly and impartially. This is not an ordinary case, as I've said so many times, and this is an extraordinary woman who made some mistakes for which she has agreed to pay, and has already paid."

While Bob Brass chewed on that, his face twisting into a scowl, the judge turned to me.

"You will report to the Middlesex County Adult Correction Center on Monday morning at nine o'clock," he instructed. "If you do not appear, a warrant will issue for your arrest. If you do not appear, I'm going to suggest to Mr. Brass that you be indicted for fourth-degree contempt of court. That's an eighteen-month sentence. And I can guarantee you I will give you an extended term on it. You understand me?"

"Yes, Your Honor," I replied, getting to my feet quickly, and then everyone else around me did the same. Before I knew what was happening, the judge was excusing himself from the bench and retiring to his chamber, and the hearing was over. I looked at Rob, who was talking quietly to Melissa.

"That's it?" I asked him. "Is it over?"

"It's over, Ellyn," he said, smiling at me and putting a hand on my arm, squeezing it reassuringly. "It's over."

Just hearing those words caused a knot to form in my throat, and I put a hand up over my mouth to try to hold in the sob that I knew was coming. *It's over,* I repeated in my head, unable for the moment to even comprehend the words. *It's over.* I wondered how many times I would have to say it before it sank in.

"Ellyn." Behind me, my husband's voice broke into my thoughts and pulled me back to reality, and I turned around and practically leapt into his arms.

"It's over," I told him, still trying to convince myself, and then I said the same to both of my daughters, and to Michael Kaufman, and to every single person who had come out to support me that day. I hugged all of them one by one, crying my eyes out and thanking them over and over, and by the time I was done, I had almost convinced myself that this really *was* it. That there was nothing left to do but serve out my jail time.

When my family and I walked out of the courtroom that day, I was smiling and laughing, and my heart felt lighter than it had in a very long time. This had been the happiest day of my working life in four and a half very long, very tiring years. At long last, and at such a cost, I finally felt vindicated.

Twenty

I had three days before I had to turn myself in and begin my jail sentence, and the countdown began the minute I left the courthouse. *What should I take care of first?* I wondered as my husband drove us home. I made some mental lists in my head— friends I had to call, bills I had to pay, details I had to go over with my husband so he could tend to them in my absence. So much to do, so little time. I was bound to forget something in the process.

But did it matter? I wasn't going away for life, just three months. Still, staring out the car window, watching the scenery fly by on the parkway, I began to think, *This is the last time I'll drive home, the last time I'll see planes flying overhead, the last time I'll pass through this toll both.* I couldn't help it. I almost laughed at the drama of it.

But really, it wasn't funny. Sure it was only three months, but *I was going to jail.* And not just jail but *prison.* Though I'd been on a bit of a high once I'd heard the judge say that he'd give me the minimum sentence and recommend me for ISP, now that things had quieted down, the reality of it was setting in. The sentence was definitely not as bad as it could have been, but it was still jail time, and I had no idea what to expect. Would I be harassed? Would I be safe? I'd just taken a self-defense course and now wondered if I'd actually have to use what I'd learned. I certainly hoped not, but I was scared.

More than that, I was relieved that the schools would live on and that everything would be over very soon. But I wasn't quite ready to deal with what would happen to me in the long run. I could only take it one step at a time.

"Just focus on Monday," I told myself as we pulled the car into the driveway in front of our house, and I got out and stretched my arms and legs. I was tired in both body and mind, and though I'd made all those lists of things I had to attend to, all I really wanted to do was take a nap. I checked my watch; it was nearing four o'clock. I wondered if I could just lie down for a few minutes.

Once in the house, though, I realized that it wouldn't be possible. The phone was ringing as we opened the door, and there were already five other messages on the answering machine. Friends and family who hadn't been able to attend the hearing were calling to hear about what had happened or, as I found out, to tell me what the press was saying had happened. Though I was incredibly media shy after the fiasco with the attorney general's press release regarding my allocution, I fired up the computer and Googled my name again. This time, the results were not any better.

"Head of Private Education Services Corporation Sentenced to Prison for Fraudulently Overbilling Districts $1.3 Million" read the headline on the attorney general's latest press release. Reading that word again—*fraudulently*—I began to feel sick to my stomach. Scanning the document, I got as far as the fourth paragraph before I had to stop reading:

> In pleading guilty, Lerner admitted that High Road, which has its principal offices in Sayreville, and Kids 1 fraudulently overbilled New Jersey school districts $1,332,247 between July 1, 2001 and Oct. 19, 2004 for sending students to their four special education schools.

"No, I didn't," I said weakly. I was so tired of this game. I had never admitted to *fraudulently* doing anything. How could they keep saying that I did? I had the transcripts of the entire court process and "fraud" did not appear in it once. Had these members of the press been in the same courtroom I'd been in? Had they heard the judge's sympathy toward me? Had they heard him force the prosecutor to say there had been no fraud, just misconduct and a mistake in judgment?

No, it seemed, they hadn't. Once again, they'd simply printed the AG's press release, which, judging by its time and date stamp, had been written prior to the court appearance to begin with.

Picking up the phone, I dialed Rob Kipnees at his office.

"They're at it again," I told him when he answered. "Can't we sue them or something? To get them to stop saying I committed *fraud?*"

On the other end of the line, Rob asked me to hold on a minute, then asked whomever was in his office to excuse him so he could take my call. God bless him, he always made time for me, for all my questions and rants and complaints.

"Ellyn, what good would that do?" he asked, as always, calmly and patiently. "Think this through. This isn't a legal document. It's a press release. And *fraudulently* is merely an adjective. They're not convicting you of it. It's just a descriptive word that the public will understand."

"But it's *wrong*," I countered, struggling to keep my voice as steady as his. "They're manipulating the language, just like they've done all along, to make me look like a bad guy. They misconstrued the facts, the law and the case. They never had enough of a real case against me, so they've made things up and screwed everyone's words around until they sounded like something horrible."

"You're right, they have. But consider this, Ellyn: As of today, the process is over. Do you really want to start on a whole new legal journey that might cost you another small fortune? And to what avail? I can't guarantee any fundamental degree of success in this instance as much as I could in the case against New Road, had it gone to trial. These publications are misleading their readers, that's all. This is no longer a case of legality. It's now an issue of ethics and the press does not have moral rules of procedure. The political and legal systems have long and very well-known histories of killing an ant with a sledgehammer and then justifying it to the press. Look at Martha Stewart."

"Or Arthur Anderson," I offered.

"Yes. The government tried to build a case against two or three employees there who were following their own company's shredding policies, and it completely overreached. The company was destroyed and all its shareholders and its eighty-five thousand innocent employees had to bear the dire consequences."

I'd still been scrolling through the press release as he spoke, absently reading it again, but now I stopped, and I closed the laptop to put it to sleep. I just didn't want to see it anymore, didn't want to deal with any of it.

"This is the worst thing that has happened to me in my life, these press releases," I said.

Rob laughed once. "Really?" he asked. "Worse than going to prison?"

I had to think about it for a moment. "Well, ask me in three months. But I'm pretty sure my answer will be the same. Rob, I've taken everything else they've thrown at me and I think I've done so pretty admirably, but these... This public defamation, the societal condemnation... I don't know. It's just more than I can take. Once the public thinks you're a crook, there's no changing their minds. I'm never going to be able to work in education again. No one will work with me after this. I'll always be a criminal now."

"No, you won't, Ellyn," Rob was quick to disagree. "You'll still be the same amazing person you've always been. And if anyone can find a way to the bright side out of all of this, it's you. I know you'll eventually make something good of it."

Now it was my turn to laugh, but the sound was dry and painful in my throat. "Thanks, Rob," I said. "I hope you're right." And then I bid him goodbye for the time being. I was sure I'd be calling him again soon, whenever the next wave of panic hit.

On Saturday, I returned phone calls and emails and caught up with all the people I would miss while I was away. On Sunday, I went over everything in the house with my husband and daughters, making sure that someone knew where I kept my checkbook, the password to my computer and every other detail I could think of that they might need in my absence. I probably overloaded them; by the end of the day, they all looked like they'd run a marathon.

I felt bad about putting all this responsibility on everyone else's shoulders, and I was actually pretty sure they would all survive just fine for the three months of my incarceration. The problem was that if I stopped for just a minute, if I ceased giving directions, I'd have to think about the fact that I wouldn't be able to hug any of them for an entire ninety days or whether or not they'd be able to visit me together. And if I thought about that, I would have lost it. So as usual, I just kept on going. It was the only way for me to survive.

By the time the sun rose on Monday morning, I was wiped out and frankly, quite ready to surrender. I'd run myself ragged all weekend and had barely slept; I felt exhausted and sick and weak. Still, I was hopeful; at least the legal wrangling was over, so there would be no more hearings, no more investigation. I was going to jail, but this was the end of the process. The horrible part of the ordeal was over. Now I just had to bide my time and wait out the last of it.

Because how bad was jail going to be, really? I didn't know much about the local institutions but I couldn't imagine that I would be sent to some sort of high-security facility full of murderers and armed robbers. There had to be a jail for people like me—older, less violent, more white-collar. I wasn't expecting whatever country club Martha Stewart had undoubtedly been sentenced to, but there had to be something in the middle that would be right for me. At least, I prayed to God that there would be.

What I found, however, when I arrived at the Middlesex County Adult Correction Center—a sort of holding pen where I'd be kept for two weeks until my transfer to the state prison—was that despite the judge's assertion that I wasn't any ordinary defendant, in the eyes of the penal system, I *was* just another criminal. From the moment I set foot in the place, I was not Dr. Ellyn Lerner, former CEO of New Road Schools, educator and innovator, esteemed member of the New Jersey special education community, wife, mother and dear friend. I was an inmate, and my identification number was the only thing that made me unique.

After a quick but tearful goodbye to my husband and daughters, I was escorted into the correction center's intake room, where I was fingerprinted and photographed, then unceremoniously told to undress. Upon the instructions of my lawyer I had brought nothing with me but the clothes on my back and now I even had to surrender those. Under the watchful eyes of not one but three different guards—all women, thankfully, but strangers nonetheless—I stripped down to nothing and handed over the last vestige of personal protection that I had. I won't even mention the humiliating body search I had to endure.

The same guard who had taken my picture grabbed my clothes from me and mashed them up into a ball, then shoved them in a small box that would be mailed to my house. Another guard handed me my uniform: green pants and a top similar to medical scrubs along with three pairs of underwear, two bras and a nightgown. Completing the package were two towels, a set of scratchy sheets, a thin blanket and a small, nylon laundry bag—how big did it have to be, really? I had nothing. Last, she handed me a tiny toothbrush with no handle, just a loop that would fit around my index finger, so I couldn't, I assume, use it as a weapon.

All these new belongings in hand, and dressed in my uniform, I followed one of the guards out of the intake room and down a corridor lined with cells. I tried not to look too far inside their barred doors—among the advice my well-meaning friends gave me was "don't look people in the eye"; I was also told not to buy anything for other inmates in the commissary once I was allowed to have money and basically just not to trust anyone. I'd been paranoid enough before those conversations, sure that I was going to get verbally or physically roughed up on a regular basis. Once I heard all that, my fear just got a whole lot worse.

When we got to my cell, one guard made me stand back while the other unlocked the door, and then I was allowed inside. Of course I hadn't been expecting much, but the space was much smaller even than I'd expected. There were two beds, one on top of the other, one toilet, one sink. A recessed fluorescent light in the ceiling. The cinderblock walls were painted a dull gray.

At least it's clean, I thought, slowly walking in and setting my things down on the lower bunk.

"Do I have a…a roommate?" I asked the guard, who was already slamming the cell door behind me. I cringed when the metal bars clanked closed against the wall.

"She's at work," the guard said, sounding bored, not even looking at me, then just walked off back down the corridor, leaving me completely alone.

Twenty-One

All told, the two weeks in the county jail went pretty quickly and much more easily than I'd thought they would. My cellmate, when she returned, turned out to be not so bad; she was there for a DWI charge, like many of them were. That or drugs, both of which carried a mandatory ninety-day sentence followed by ninety days in rehab. I felt for these women. They'd made some bad choices—and had some bad choices thrust upon them—and were paying their dues. Without all the chemicals in their systems, they were really pretty nice.

Since I was, in essence, just a visitor there, I wasn't given a job like my cellmate, who would serve out her entire sentence there. I just lay on my bed, staring at the ceiling, thinking back on the last almost five years of my life, imagining how things could have turned out differently if only, if only, if only… I tortured myself with hypotheticals to pass the time.

And that took up the better part of an hour or two. Honestly, I'd spent so much time preparing myself for this incarceration that once I was there and settled in—once I saw that I would be safe—I moved my mind on to other things. This was the first time in a very, very long time that I had no responsibilities whatsoever, not for my family or my job or anything. The only thing I had to focus on was me, and despite the surroundings, I was sort of looking forward to it. I needed this time to regroup…and catch up on my reading. All my friends sent me books. Over those two weeks I finished seven in total.

When it was time for my transfer, the same three guards who had checked me in to the facility came back and took away all the stuff they had given me—the extra underwear, the bed sheets, even the little fingertip toothbrush. I gave all the books I'd read away to the other avid readers in the area, who really seemed to appreciate the gesture. Then, the guards led me back down the corridor to the intake room. This time, as we walked, I glanced inside the other cells along the way, saying quick goodbyes to all the women I had managed to meet, realizing that all the stories I'd heard about incarcerated women had been wrong. I wished each of them well on their journeys, and they wished me well in return.

In the intake room, a guard fitted me with wrist and ankle cuffs and wove the chains that connected them into a communal shackle with five other inmates—two I'd already met, three I didn't know. I began to get that old feeling in the pit of my stomach, the fear and dread of the unknown. I'd made somewhat of a success out of this first two-week stay by treating my fellow inmates with kindness and humanity. All so many of them needed was someone to listen, and I'd been nothing in my life if not a sympathetic ear. But would that do me any good when I got to the big house?

Packed on a bright-blue school bus with "Middlesex County Department of Corrections" emblazoned down the side in big, white letters, I folded my still-shackled hands in my lap and looked down at them. Some of the women on that bus were rough, angry; I guessed that they'd been convicted of something more serious than corporate misconduct, maybe even more serious than DWI or drugs. I quietly hoped that none of them would be my cellmate. And then I felt bad for being scared of them.

Because people are people—wasn't that what I'd spent most of my life trying to tell the world? All you have to do is treat people like human beings, with dignity and respect, and no matter what their situation is in life they will respond in kind. I knew that; I'd witnessed that. I knew this valuable lesson so well. It had truly been the basis of my career, during which I'd helped so many people and touched so many lives, not just my students but my associates, the people I worked with, parents, administrators, teachers, assistants, therapists and acquaintances. All those letters these people had written to the judge for me, all those who'd come to the hearing. For a moment, I felt a surge of euphoria. It *had* all been worth it. What I'd done *had* mattered.

I opened my eyes. The woman next to me, the one I was shackled to, was mumbling to herself. I leaned closer, trying to hear.

"Gonna throw up," I heard her say.

"Gina, are you alright?" I asked. She did look a little pale.

"Carsick," she said, stifling a burp. As the ride went on, she continued muttering about her queasiness, to the point where I was more afraid of being vomited upon than I was about going to the prison. I was chained to this woman; if she lost her breakfast, I had no way to escape.

Swallowing hard, I looked straight ahead, out the front window of the bus. Up ahead, the Edna Mahan Correctional Facility for Women loomed, and I couldn't have felt more grateful. Formerly a home for unwed mothers in the early 1900s, it was now the only women's prison in New Jersey and from the distance, it looked like a college campus. When we drove through the grounds I saw groups of women walking from one building to another, from their quarters to the mess hall, classes and their jobs. They really looked like a bunch of co-eds—except that no one carried any books, and everyone wore the same beige uniform.

At the back of the campus we drove through a gate and into the maximum-security area, which was surrounded by barbed-wire fences. Every new inmate was taken to "max," as it was known, regardless of her crime; it was like the intake center of the prison, and I would spend two weeks there. Peering out the window of the bus as it crawled to a stop outside a set of large, heavy metal doors, I swallowed hard. This would be my home for the next three months.

The prison's initial intake room looked just like the one in the county jail except larger; the strip search was basically the same, as was the uniform, except this one was beige. When the formalities were through and I'd been assigned my new ID number—620676; I will never forget it—a guard handed me my supplies: a bar of soap, a bottle of shampoo, two towels, the same sort of finger toothbrush I'd had at the county jail, toothpaste, a comb, several packets of laundry soap and some sanitary napkins, which I didn't need but took anyway. I later found that they made good heel cushions inside my prison-issue boots. They also gave us several sheets of paper, a pencil and three postage stamps, so we could write and send letters.

Anything else we wanted or needed—toiletries, clothing, food,

whatever—would have to be ordered from the commissary or borrowed from other inmates, who were, to my great surprise, very kindly
accommodating to new inmates whose commissary orders had not yet
come in. Once the orders did come in, they were still generous, but the
interest rates increased exponentially—if you borrowed, for example,
a bag of chips, you'd have to buy them two in your next commissary
order.

Because it was apparent, once I was in the general population, that
I had money to order whatever I wanted, some of my fellow inmates did
come to me, looking to borrow. Others warned me against it, telling me
that these borrowers were nothing but beggars and would never repay
me. However, I always ordered more than I needed with the sole intention of giving it away. Some of these women were truly disadvantaged,
and I wanted to help them. And they always seemed to appreciate the
help. They promised to pay me back when they could—it would be a
while, considering prison jobs paid only $2.40 an hour—but I never
took it.

That situation, however, was far off in the distance. I was still in
intake and processing and knew nothing yet about borrowers, the
commissary or the gap that existed between the haves and have-nots
even in prison.

After doling out my supplies, one of the intake guards led me
outside and toward another building—a gym surrounded by more
barbed-wire fencing. My mind flashed back to the day of the raid at
our offices in Parlin, when that cop had escorted me to the gym where
my employees were corralled. Just as it had begun, so now it ended. If I
weren't so miserable, I might have laughed at the irony.

Inside the gym, a grid of beds spread out across the floor—fifty-
four in all, most occupied already by other female inmates. The guard
on duty—this was the afternoon shift—led me over to my assigned
bunk and explained the rules.

"This is reception," she said as I gingerly placed my sheets and
clothing on the indicated cot. "This is the holding tank for all new
inmates whether you're going to minimum or maximum security. If a
guard says 'on your beds,' that means you stay on your bunk. 'Off bed'
means you can socialize or go in the common area of the gymnasium
to watch TV, or you can stay on your bunk if you want to. If you all get
too noisy off bed, the guards will send you back to your bunks."

I nodded in silence, looking around me. It was on-bunk time at the moment. I wondered what the other inmates had done to lose their privileges.

"We do head counts at six in the morning, nine-thirty, eleven-thirty, two-thirty in the afternoon, four o'clock and eight o'clock at night," the guard went on. She sounded bored, like she'd made this speech a million times. "When a guard yells out 'five to count,' you have five minutes to get back to your bunk for the count. That means drop whatever you're doing and get yourself back here. Count is serious. You have to stay completely silent while the guards are doing the count. When they say 'count clear,' you can go back to whatever you were doing. Understood?"

"Yes," I said. "Thanks."

And then without another word, the guard left me, pausing to chat with a couple other inmates on her way out. She seemed decent enough. Not friendly—none of the guards in reception were—but nothing like what you saw in the movies. Sitting on my bed, I looked around again, feeling a little like I was in the *Twilight Zone*. Prison was a big, open room full of cots. Like a sleepover. I had to take some time to wrap my mind around it.

Reception, I came to figure out, was really just a big a fishbowl; we were watched 24/7, the guards trying to scare us into submission, to tame us so we'd be docile when we moved on to our permanent assignments. Not a troublemaker to begin with, I had no troubles during my two weeks there. In fact, I found it pretty boring. More lying on a bed again, staring at the ceiling, or slumping in a plastic chair, reading or watching bad TV. At least there was a library with a surprising number of interesting books. Without them, the boredom would have been crippling. I read for almost ten hours every day and finished another six or seven books. Reading as much as I could get my hands on became my new pursuit, my new goal.

Finally, after two weeks in reception—which marked one total month of incarceration—I was brought to my final destination: the minimum-security area of the prison, where I would serve out the remaining two months of my sentence. Though I'd imagined there'd be long rows of dark, dank cells, haunted, tortured faces staring out from behind the bars, the grounds, as my area was known, was remarkably better than that. There were no bars; there weren't even any cells.

Instead we had cubicles, two inmates in each, in buildings called cottages—eight of them, six wings apiece and ten women per wing. There weren't even any locks on any of the doors.

In my cubicle, I found the standard two beds, one on each side, each with a foot locker underneath for storage. Two upright lockers stood side by side between the beds. This space wasn't as depressing as the county jail had been, and there was more privacy than I'd had in reception. It was prison, still, there could be no mistake about that, but for the first time since I'd entered the system I didn't feel an overwhelming sense of dread. I almost began to feel like I could survive it.

Though most of the women in minimum security were twenty-five to thirty-five years old, my cottage housed all older offenders like myself. Just as it had been in the county jail, many, many of them were in there for drunk driving or drug charges—for possession, or for refusing to testify against a male friend who'd gotten them involved in a drug transaction. I met so many women there who were involved in situations like that, it was almost shocking to me. Also surprising was their willingness to talk about their crimes. Without even asking, I learned who had been addicted to street drugs and who had been forging prescriptions, who was a repeat offender and who was there for the first time. There was one lone woman who'd been convicted as a madam, and out of curiosity, I would have loved to hear her story. Unfortunately, she was Asian and barely spoke English.

In the prison, unlike in the jail, I had a work assignment—the early shift in the kitchen, stacking clean meal trays as they came out of the dishwasher after breakfast and lunch. It was a pleasingly mindless job, and as a bonus I had access to all the fresh fruit I wanted.

On an average day I finished work at 1:00 p.m., then went back to my cottage to shower—it was a good time to go then because there was only one shower facility per each wing of ten women, and at most other times, there was a line. After that I either did my laundry or went to call my family, which I did every day at some point. The calling system in prison was complex—each inmate was allowed two hours of phone time per month to each phone number called, with a ten-minute limit per call. My family had to scrounge up every number they could—cell phones, home lines, work extensions—and prepay a set amount on each number so they could accept charges to any one I called. This was the only way that we were able to talk at any length.

On top of the restrictive time limits per call and per phone number, there was the cost involved as well: All calls had to be collect *and* prepaid by a tele-system that gouged inmates to the tune of one dollar a minute. That was prohibitively expensive for the families of many of the women there, who were of modest means at best. I was fortunate that my husband, daughters and friends were able to accept all my calls. My heart went out to the women who couldn't afford to speak to their children.

Some days, when I had the time and the inclination, I went to the beauty parlor on the grounds, where we could use our commissary funds to get haircuts—just cuts, mind you, not color. That would have been changing our appearances, and the Department of Corrections wouldn't allow that. Never mind that so many women had dyed hair that grew out to their natural colors during incarceration—wasn't that changing their appearance as well?

At any rate, the salon was actually a career-training facility and given my programs at New Road—the dental lab, the eye lab, the Main Street shops, all the areas that had helped get me into this mess in the first place—the idea of it interested me greatly. I was only there for three months and so didn't need my hair done too often, but I went a few times just to support the project. The women working in the beauty parlor put in their hours and learned the trade, though conviction and incarceration prohibited them from taking the licensing exam—another of the system's perverse twists.

When everything else was done for the day, I returned to my bunk and read my books. When I ran through the prison library's selections, I had friends and family mail me more; my own personal library was impressive, imposing and inspiring. The monotonous routine of prison life gave me the chance to catch up on books I'd always wanted to read but never had the time to, and when my sentence was through I really felt that I accomplished something I never would have otherwise.

When I didn't have my nose in a book, I spent my time trying to find ways to help my fellow inmates. If I had to be in prison, I figured, I would make the most of it—I would find some reason, some justification, for this fate I'd been handed. Certainly, I hadn't been sentenced to serve any sort of justice. But if I could somehow improve the lives of the women around me, maybe it would mean something.

So, I started with helping them write letters to their public defenders, mostly having to do with the inmates' children. How were they going to support them from prison, who would take care of them while they were incarcerated—a whole host of complicated issues I'd thankfully never had to consider in my own life. One woman I helped had been arrested in the first place because her mother had been taking care of her children, and she'd failed to pay child support to her mother. I couldn't imagine being incarcerated for such a thing; I also couldn't believe that her mother would press charges against her. What tough lives some of these women had. So many of their stories really tore at my heartstrings.

From letter writing, I went on to tutoring. In the prison system, anyone who hadn't graduated from high school was required to work toward a GED—I actually had a great deal of respect for the prison system for this, for giving these women the time and resources they needed to better themselves. Once it got out that I'd been a teacher, many of the women flocked to me for help with algebra and reading, mostly, two of the most troublesome subjects. At first it was just a random request here and there, but before I knew it, I was running a bona fide study group. Except for when *American Idol* was on, of course. Nothing got done anywhere on those nights.

Many of the women I tutored seemed to really regard me as their teacher—they even called me "Miss Ellyn"—and I have to admit, it was nice being back in that role again. I even enjoyed it when some of them tried to whine their way out of attending the study group or found excuses for not doing their homework. They weren't my kids, so I couldn't tell them that there'd be no TV until they finished their homework. I had to be more creative than that. I would figure out some bargain to offer them for doing at least half of their assignments with me each evening—for example, do one more page of these factoring problems and I'll finish your last page. The more they did themselves, under my supervision, the more they began to understand, and the more of their homework assignment I would offer to do for them. I found that they would often put forth much more effort on their difficult assignments if I offered to ghostwrite a paragraph or two on the easier ones.

Overall, this tutoring was fantastic to me. It wasn't like running New Road, and it wasn't exactly the population I had chosen to teach, but it felt so damned good to be helping people again, to be a productive member of this little microcosm of society. It also helped me re-realize the true importance of education and how grossly undervalued it is in America. If only these women had been given more opportunities earlier in their lives, I thought. If only they'd had a place like New Road. If only they'd had teachers who had turned them on to learning—or at least bargained with them as I did to complete their work. Maybe they would have ended up very differently.

All in all, by the time the end of my three-month stint came around, I was back to feeling pretty okay with things. I'd used my time in prison wisely, as a respite from the normally huge amount of responsibility I shouldered in my life, and done my best to remain positive, grateful, appreciative and even joyful despite my surroundings. I had such an upbeat attitude, in fact, that one woman told me I looked like I was on a spa retreat, not locked up in prison. That was funny—there was certainly nothing spa-like about our surroundings.

But, I could see what she meant. I did use my time there to regroup mentally and reset my priorities. No matter how despondent I became, I held fast to the knowledge that I was doing the right thing for New Road. I felt good about that; the knowledge gave me power. It also got me through many rough times and launched me over the enormous hurdle of embarrassment that the investigation, the sentencing and the awful media coverage had put before me. It also helped me, in the end, realize some very important lessons:

How you treat people is everything.

To build something bigger than yourself, you have to sacrifice.

Never, ever abandon your convictions.

And life is a test.

On the day I was released from prison, I knew I had passed. I had no clue what I was going to do with my life, but I felt prepared to face whatever would await me.

Twenty-Two

Though my time in prison was surprisingly acceptable, even pleasant, at the end of my three-month term I was more than ready to go home. I missed my family, of course, and longed for creature comforts and familiar surroundings—my favorite reading chair in front of the gas fireplace in the living room, my favorite coffee cup, my laptop, my cell phone, a luxurious bubble bath. One more thing I learned from my prison stay was just how much I had taken things like that for granted. Whoever said that you don't know what you have until it's gone was telling the truth.

However, before I could get back to the life I knew—or, at least, whatever was left of it—there was one more obstacle to face: a three-judge panel that would decide if I was ready to be released. I was scheduled to stand before them on January 21, 2009. Though the sentencing judge had given me the minimum and I'd been accepted into the intensive supervision program, which would keep tabs on me once I was released, I still had to go through these formalities. There was no way I wouldn't be released.

At least, that was what I thought until I stood before the panel.

"I'm not sure that white-collar criminals truly understand how serious their offenses are," said one of the judges from behind his table. He was flanked by another male judge on the left, a female judge on the right. I stood behind another table about six feet in front of them, next to my lawyer, Rob Kipnees. I had shackles on my ankles and wrists. Each of the judges looked at me stoically, their expressions not telling me anything about what they thought of me.

Turning my head, I looked at my lawyer, whose face did give me a message: *Keep quiet.* He knew me too well. I looked back to the front of the room.

"I'm not even sure this candidate understands that she committed a crime at all," the same judge went on, glancing sideways at his colleagues. I shifted my weight from one foot to the other, as much as the leg irons would let me. I hadn't been expecting this reception at all. I'd figured they'd tell me what a model prisoner I was and call for my immediate release. It hadn't even occurred to me that they could make me stay in prison longer.

"You may be seated," the second male judge said, then he and the others went into a huddle. Rob and I sat down behind our table.

"I think they hate me. Can they hate me just from looking at my paperwork?" I whispered to him, one eye on the front of the room.

He laughed a little. "No, that's how they play it with every inmate who comes before them. It's just intimidation—like good cop/bad cop. They want you to see that they're serious. Don't let it get to you."

"Alright," I said. Up at the panel's table the judges continued their powwow. I turned around in my seat a little and smiled at my husband and daughters in the first row of the audience. Behind them were my brother, Richie, and his wife, Elaine, my husband's sister, Debbie, and her husband, Neil, and Mort Plawner, a friend who had volunteered to be one of my two community ISP sponsors. This meant that he could vouch for me if I for some reason derailed and went outside of the ISP regulations.

"Ms. Lerner," the female judge said, and I turned back around to face the courtroom.

I stood. "Yes, Your Honor."

She smiled at me. This was the good cop. "You are aware of the seriousness of your crime." She said it as a statement, not a question.

"Yes, Your Honor," I repeated.

Glancing down at some papers on the table in front of her, she went on. "Well, your paperwork is in excellent condition, and I recommend immediate release. Our vote is unanimous."

I felt my knees go weak; I grabbed the edge of the table to support myself. Behind me, I could hear my family quietly rejoicing. Rob put a hand on my shoulder.

"See?" he said, smiling at me. "I told you there was nothing to worry about."

Everything that happened after that is sort of a blur to me now. My shackles were removed, and I was allowed to hug my husband and children. And before I knew it, I was in the car. On the way home, I cried. It was done; the whole ordeal was now entirely in the past. Now, it was just a matter of building my future.

My ISP officer was named Denise, and she was a decent woman. She seemed to understand that I was not a hardened criminal and that I was willing to abide by whatever rules were laid down for me, so she went as easy on me as she could while still enforcing the program's requirements. Those included weekly urine testing for drugs and even drinking, which was not allowed under ISP; sometimes Denise or another ISP officer showed up randomly at my house with a little plastic cup, too. She assured me that this was standard procedure, not that she suspected I was under the influence.

The requirements also included a six o'clock curfew, and I couldn't have a cell phone until I found a job. Fortunately, my friend Lee had a corporate education company she'd built herself and she agreed to extend employment to me starting in February. I wrote training curricula and proposals for her firm's workshops, though I couldn't actually teach at any of them; they usually lasted for two or three day offsite and I couldn't leave the state or stay out past my curfew.

If the firm sold the programs that were based on the materials I wrote—on topics such as leadership under adversity and emotional intelligence—it would generate royalties for me. That was good, but in an ideal world, this really wasn't the job I would have chosen. It was education-related, in a way, but it wasn't New Road. It wasn't working with my kids or the people I'd trained and nurtured to become the best they could be. Still, it fulfilled my ISP requirements, and so I was grateful to my friend for the opportunity. It was enough to help me regain my footing and get used to working again.

For five months I worked out of my house, which only increased my sense of isolation from my former life and the world I once knew, and before long that started to take a toll on me. It had been too long since I'd felt like an involved and engaged member of society, since I'd felt the passion for and commitment to my work that I used to experience every day.

Thanks to the declining economy, as time went on Lee barely had enough work for herself and her full-time staff. It became very difficult for them to sell new programs to new clients and I knew even my small base salary was a burden to her. So, in May, I resigned and started looking for other options.

Under the plea agreement I couldn't own a company or even apply for credit while under ISP, so while I had plenty of ideas, my ability to execute them was extremely limited...but not completely out of reach. I've always believed that if there's a will, there's a way, and while I was bound to follow the ISP regulations and requirements—there was no way I would do anything that would land me back in prison—I also wasn't content just to sit at home and do nothing. Nor would ISP allow me to do so.

The most viable idea I had at the time came about through some conversations with Dr. Michael Kaufman, the CEO of SESI, or Specialized Education Services, Inc., the company that now operated the High Road Schools in Connecticut, Maryland, Delaware, Rhode Island and Washington, DC. As part of my plea agreement with the New Jersey Division of Criminal Justice, New Road of New Jersey had been sold to an employee stock ownership plan in September 2008 and been completely disassociated from the out-of-state entities.

Mike Kaufman, who had written such a wonderful letter to the sentencing judge on my behalf, had taken charge of SESI about two years before I'd gone into prison and while I'd known he was a great operational leader, he turned out to be the most phenomenal educational and business leader as well. Under his tenure, SESI grew tremendously powerful, profitable and increasingly dedicated to making an impact on the students and in the field of education within the states in which it operated. Though at first I'd been a little bit sad to see my life's work turned over to someone else, when I saw Mike take the foundation I'd created and triple its growth in three years, I understood what it meant: it was time for me to step back so that my enterprise could be catapulted into greatness. I'd prayed for that sort of success, and the universe indeed answered me by putting Michael Kaufman in charge of the company.

As far as New Road in New Jersey, I was equally sad to leave my position there behind, but that organization benefited from the transition as well. Falling under the capable leadership of Annette Hockenjos,

New Road has continued to run as the well-oiled, high-quality machine it has always been, and my leaving it has felt nothing but right. I truly believe that everything happens for a reason, and my departure meant that my schools could move on to the next chapter. It was time for that—and time for me to do the same.

And so, in June 2009, that was what I did. While talking to Mike about SESI, I learned that the company had eighteen current leases for its facilities, six of which would expire within four years; most would expire within seven. My idea, then, was to get into the real estate business and actually own the properties that SESI used—in essence, to be its landlord. Of course, I couldn't own such a business myself, so I got some family members involved, including my brother, who would be president of this new company, and my daughter, who is a lawyer and could handle the legal aspects of it.

Because every move I made in life had to be approved by ISP first, I wrote up a document outlining this plan as well as the company's potential—a sort of mini business plan that I submitted to Denise. She ran it through the appropriate channels and eventually gave me the go-ahead to start the company. I was installed as chief operating officer.

Initially, our intention was to purchase one to three school buildings per year and lease them to SESI or its subsidiaries or divisions so that we would own ten properties by 2014. We've been running the business just under a year and so far, we've acquired only one new property in Sacramento, but we also count among our holdings the school properties I already owned in Washington, DC, Maryland and New Jersey.

Although working in school real estate is not as intense or rewarding as being involved in school operations, at least I'm out there again, doing my thing. I also have my family and friends, a good home and good health and a sense of stability in my life again. I can't complain about much—or, at least, I won't. Complaining, I've found, gets you nowhere. The only thing that moves you ahead in life is pushing onward, and I try to do that every day.

Of course, I would love to be back in the business of helping students and training teachers, or at least somehow working in the special education field. This real estate job is education-related, but I'm on the periphery, really. What I'm doing now is a living, but it's not my passion.

Someday, when I'm ready, when the right idea hits me, I will move on to something else. Something big, something great, something important, something that calls me. I just don't know yet what it will be.

———

When I began writing this book in April 2009, I was feeling very lost, like I would never amount to anything ever again. I was terrified that I would never achieve success like I had at New Road, never again affect people's lives for the better, as I had there. What a difference a year makes, though. At this point, I am ready for anything—and, more importantly, *open* to anything.

Part of this comes from the fact that I can look back and see what I went through, and that I survived. My entire life was turned upside down and inside out and I have lived to tell the tale. That alone is pretty empowering. But it also has to do with what I can only describe as a spiritual awakening, spurred by a letter that I received from Laibel Schapiro, the rabbi of my synagogue, while I was in prison. In the letter, he talked to me about the Torah passage known as "Lech Lecha," or "Go Out," in which G-d instructed Abraham to take leave of his native land and travel "to the land that I will show you."

The rabbi wrote:

> "Lech Lecha" is G-d's beckoning call to Abraham—and by extension to each one of us—to always look ahead and strive to grow through the challenges and adversities that we encounter in our journeys. These adversities should not be seen merely as setbacks but as opportunities to bring ourselves to newer and better places in life. Every descent is only for the sake of a greater ascent.
>
> After Abraham heeded G-d's instruction and made his way to the land of Canaan, a famine broke out, forcing Abraham to journey yet again—this time to the land of Egypt, where Sarah was taken captive by Pharoah. While no harm befell her during her imprisonment, the episode was nonetheless a very difficult and traumatic ordeal for both Sarah and Abraham. It

was undoubtedly a descent of painful proportions that enabled them to achieve a much greater ascent than might ever have been attained otherwise. By the time they returned to Canaan, they had accumulated cattle, silver and gold as well as knowledge and experience.

When I first read this—and still today; I pull the letter out when I'm feeling unsure of myself—it struck such a chord within me. "Lech Lecha" truly captured the essence of what being a member of the family of Abraham and Sarah is all about, and I'd lost sight of that. In the midst of the accusations and investigation, through the meetings with lawyers and the plea agreement and the hearings and prison and probation, I'd forgotten the most fundamental requirement of the Jewish faith: being always ready to "go out"—to leave my comfort zone and journey to wherever G-d leads me, to a place where I may develop my inner potential and accomplish great things. When I began to think this way, it was easier for me to see that I didn't have to let what had happened ruin me; that I had a choice in where I ended up in life, no matter what setbacks I had to endure; and that I could even use those setback as springboards from which to reach greater heights. After a wounding, I learned, you find your greatest story.

While no one welcomes or relishes the trials and tribulations of life, especially those that condemn us and ostracize us from our rightful places in society, it is precisely as Rabbi Schapiro wrote in his letter to me:

> When circumstances outside of ourselves become most trying and overwhelming, we must search deep within ourselves, to our very souls, and find the inner reservoir of strength and faith that tells us that just beyond this temporary darkness is a radiant light—a new light, a brighter light than has ever shone upon us before.

Although I am not a religious person, I have much faith and when I first received this letter, I was on a quest for a greater sense of spirituality. Rabbi Schapiro's words elevated my spirit, my courage and my convictions to a level that I never knew would be possible, and I realized that the entire ordeal I'd gone through for the sake of the schools—for the sake of New Road—had not been for naught. Without that test, I never would have known just how much I am capable of.

―――

So, the big question is, if I had the chance, would I do it all again? Without a doubt, yes, for the reason that I just mentioned above. Going through all of that was hell, but in the end, I learned a lot from it. It was a painful but valuable experience that I wouldn't trade for the world.

However, I would not do it all exactly the same. I would still do everything I did for my schools, my students and my people; I always had all of their best interests at heart, and nothing could change that. I wouldn't, though, so flagrantly disrespect the regulations, even if they made little sense to me or even if I thought my way would produce better results for my students. I can admit that I cheated, that I skirted the rules in order to get the best for New Road. But I hadn't done it for personal gain, and so I'd thought that I could never get in trouble for it. That was naïve—I know that now.

I also now have a long list of things I will never do again. I will never again be naïve about the nature of bureaucracy. The process I went through, from investigation to incarceration, taught me one lesson over and over: if you color outside the lines, if you fly above the radar, you wear a target on your back and when you find yourself in trouble, people will believe that you only achieved greatness because you cheated in some way. It didn't matter that my practices saved taxpayers money and made New Road's tuition among the lowest in the state at a time when New Jersey was screaming at all educational institutions about saving money. It doesn't matter that these days, now that New Road follows the regulations to the letter, its tuition rate has increased seventy percent, from tenth-lowest out of 175 schools in the state to just around the median. All that matters is that I didn't follow the rules.

And I will never, ever make that mistake again. If I ever find myself in a similar situation, where I can't play by the rules or restrictions imposed by the industry in which I work, then I will leave and do something else. I no longer need to prove that my outside-the-box thinking is better than that of the average person who follows and never leads.

Next, I will never again make my organization more important than myself. Never again will I put myself in this sort of Sophie's choice, where I must choose to save either the company I've created or my own reputation. My next venture will not be as precious; it will not be my baby. It will be an adult, able to stand on its own and not requiring its mother to give up her life to keep it safe. In short, whatever I do from here on out will not be my life's work. I did that already—that was New Road. It was a third child to me and I cared more about the plight of its students and employees than I did for myself. I never took profits out of the organization; I reinvested everything back into it. And where did that get me? With my house put up as collateral for bank loans to run the schools and unable to fund my own legal defense. If I hadn't put all my eggs into the one school basket I might have been able to afford to push the case to trial, and without a doubt I would have prevailed.

Last, I will never put myself in a situation where the government can force me into something I don't want to do by threatening to damage or destroy the enterprise I've built. I did that for New Road, but New Road was unique. Never again will I be railroaded. Not for anything.

These days, my ISP is almost over, which means that my restrictions—the curfew, the ban on credit, the awful drug testing, my inability to have a glass of wine with dinner—are about to be lifted. Once I'm free, I think I might travel for a while, see the world and figure out what to do with my life. Somewhere out there, I hope to find the entrance to my second act, to find the thing that will ultimately bring me fulfillment. I know I want to operate in social services; I know I want to benefit society. I know that I definitely do not want to be government-funded. But other than that, I am open to ideas, optimistic about the future, and positive that my calling will find me.